THE SEARCH FOR A
SECOND SUIT

IT'S IN HERE SOMEWHERE

JAMES MARSH STERNBERG AND DANNY KLEINMAN

authorHOUSE

AuthorHouse™
1663 Liberty Drive
Bloomington, IN 47403
www.authorhouse.com
Phone: 833-262-8899

Published by AuthorHouse 12/02/2021

ISBN: 978-1-6655-4624-9 (sc)
ISBN: 978-1-6655-4623-2 (e)

CONTENTS

Also by James Marsh Sternberg

Playing To Trick One, No Mulligans in Bridge

Trump Suit Headaches, Rx for Declarers

The Finesse, Only a Last Resort

Blocking and Unblocking

Shortness; A Key to Better Bidding

When Michaels Meets the Unusual

Endplays and Elimination

and by James Marsh Sternberg
with Danny Kleinman:

Second Hand High, Third Hand Not Too High

An Entry, An Entry, My Kingdom For An Entry

L O L, Loser – On - Loser

The Search For A Second Suit

ACKNOWLEDGEMENTS

This book would not have been possible without the help of several friends. Frank Stewart, Michael Lawrence, Anne Lund, and Eddie Kantar, all provided suggestions for material for the book.

Jim says he is forever indebted to Hall of Famer Fred Hamilton, without whose guidance and teaching he says he could not have achieved whatever success he has had in bridge.

And he also wants to thank Vickie Lee Bader, whose love and patience helped guide him thru the many hours of this endeavor.

James Marsh Sternberg MD

Palm Beach Gardens FL

Danny Kleinman, Psephologist

Los Angeles, CA

DEDICATION

This book is dedicated to the memory of

BERNIE CHAZEN

A great teacher and player,

but an even better friend

INTRODUCTION

Becoming a good declarer starts with some basic principles. All the books tell you the same thing; before playing to Trick 1, think and form a plan. But what should you think about? Players often look at a deal and see a new mystery, a complex problem. They become overwhelmed.

Of all the ways of winning tricks, cashing high cards and taking finesses are easiest. But establishing a long suit requires effort and care. To set up intermediate cards, lose tricks you cannot avoid losing.

Most deals come down to one problem. You are usually within a trick of your contract: you must find a missing honor or get rid of a loser in a key suit. If the deal requires a criss-cross squeeze followed by an endplay that only Zia can pull off, or you are three or four tricks too high, play fast, go down, and save your energy for the next deal.

Most deals require hand-type recognition. Bridge does not reinvent itself on each deal. There are only a limited number of hand-types that repeat over and over. There may be variations on each theme, but the basic hand types remain the same. Often you will hear an expert say "I've seen this deal before." What he means is he has seen this type of deal, probably many times. Once you recognize what type of deal it is, you will usually have some idea how to proceed.

Common hand types include second suits, simple finesses, ruffing in dummy, cross-ruffing, endplays and eliminations, dummy reversals, keeping danger hands off lead, and squeezes. There are others but this covers most of what you will encounter. You have to think about timing, entries, and so forth, but once you recognize the hand type, you know which road to start down. This applies to defenders as well.

The most common type of deal is a second suit. This book will focus entirely on variations of second suit type deals. It is divided into chapters, including one on defense, but there is some overlap. I show all four hands for convenience, but try covering the hands except dummy's and your own until you have played the deal through mentally. Assume rubber bridge or IMPs, where making contracts is paramount. Don't worry about extra undertricks or overtricks. You have a big clue as to what type of deal each is. I'm not so mean as to try to sneak something else in.

CHAPTER 1
Entries

DEAL 1. WHEN TO HOLD 'EM

                    ♠ A J 5
                    ♡ 3 2
                    ◊ J 6 2
                    ♣ A Q 7 6 2
    ♠ 9 4 2   ♠ 8 6
    ♡ J 9 4   ♡ K Q 10 8 7
    ◊ A K 10 9 4   ◊ 7 5
    ♣ 9 4   ♣ J 10 8 5
                    ♠ K Q 10 7 3
                    ♡ A 6 5
                    ◊ Q 8 3
                    ♣ K 3

Playing Two-Over-One Game-Forcing ("2/1 GF"), South opened 1♠ and reached 4♠ on an uncontested auction.

The defense started with two top diamonds and a diamond ruff. South won East's ♡K return and drew trumps in three rounds. Then he tried to run clubs. He discarded one of his two low hearts on dummy's third club honor, but when clubs split 4-2 he had no place to park his other low heart.

"Just my luck," he griped as he recorded down one.

But was it? Could South have guarded against 4-2 clubs?

Yes, by planning for it. Preserving a trump entry to dummy does the job. After drawing only two rounds of trumps with the ♠A and ♠K, take the ♣K and ♣A. Then ruff a low club high.

A low trump to dummy's ♠J draws West's last trump. With West's trumps gone, dummy's ♣Q and established ♣7 provide discards for both low hearts.

DEAL 2. WHEN TO FOLD 'EM

```
              ♠ A J 5
              ♡ 3 2
              ◇ J 6 2
              ♣ A Q 7 6 2
♠ 9 6 4 2                        ♠ 8
♡ J                             ♡ K Q 10 9 8 7 4
◇ A K 10 9 4                     ◇ 7 5
♣ 9 8 4                         ♣ J 10 5
              ♠ K Q 10 7 3
              ♡ A 6 5
              ◇ Q 8 3
              ♣ K 3
```

Playing 2/1 GF, South opened 1♠ and reached 4♠ on an uncontested auction.

The defense started with two top diamonds and a diamond ruff. South won East's ♡K return.

South felt like he had seen this hand before, perhaps in a dream, but he wasn't going to make the same mistake twice. He cashed the ♠A and ♠K, leaving the ♠J as an entry in the dummy.

He played the ♣K, crossed to the ♣A and ruffed a club high. "I don't recall everyone following when I played this deal before," he mused.

He crossed to dummy's carefully-preserved ♠J but when he discarded a heart on dummy's ♣Q, West ruffed. No place to park his last heart. Down one.

"Now what did I do wrong?" wondered South. Do you know?

Perhaps he was too busy ogling the blonde kibitzer who sat Northwest. They really shouldn't allow low-cut blouses at bridge clubs. Poor South didn't notice East's heart discard on the second spade. Once trumps split 4-1, South had to pull all West's trumps and rely on 3-3 clubs.

DEAL 3. LISTEN TO THE BIDDING

```
                        ♠ Q J 3
                        ♡ 7 6
                        ◊ 9 4 2
                        ♣ A K 8 7 4
        ♠ K 4 2                         ♠ 5
        ♡ A K J 8                       ♡ 10 5 4 3 2
        ◊ Q 7                           ◊ J 10 8 5
        ♣ Q J 10 2                      ♣ 9 6 3
                        ♠ A 10 9 8 7 6
                        ♡ Q 9
                        ◊ A K 6 3
                        ♣ 5
```

East's Jacoby Transfer 2◊ response to West's strong-notrump opening didn't stop South from overcalling 2♠ despite the adverse vulnerability, nor keep North from raising to 4♠.

West cashed both top hearts and switched to the ♣Q. South shifted his gaze from Northwest: did she have to leave the top button of her blouse open? "What's the contract?" he asked.

"Four spades, Danny," answered Northwest. Kibitzers aren't supposed to answer, but everyone made an exception for this kibitzer. South took dummy's ♣K and let the ♠Q ride for a finesse.

West won the ♠K and exited in trump. Declarer threw one low diamond on dummy's ♣A but had to lose his other low diamond at the end. Down one.

Where were you looking during the auction? How would you play 4♠?

West's strong-notrump opening marks him with the ♠K, so forgo the spade finesse. Instead set up dummy's clubs for *two* diamond discards. Dummy's two spade honors provide the two entries you need.

At Trick 4, ruff a low club. Lead a low spade. If West plays low, win dummy's ♠J and ruff another club. Lead another low spade. Whether West wins or ducks, dummy's ♠Q is the entry to dummy's *two* good clubs.

DEAL 4. COMPRESSING TWELVE INTO ELEVEN

♠ K 8 3
♡ Q 7 3
♢ K 7 6 5 4
♣ 9 3

♠ 10 9 　　　　　　　　　　　♠ Q J 7 6 5
♡ A K J 9 6 5 　　　　　　　♡ 10 8 4 2
♢ Q 10 8 3 　　　　　　　　♢ 9
♣ 6 　　　　　　　　　　　　♣ 10 7 2

♠ A 4 2
♡ void
♢ A J 2
♣ A K Q J 8 5 4

Not deeming his hand quite good enough for his partnership's strong artificial 2♣ opening, and not relishing the competition in hearts that it might provoke, South opened 1♣. The opponents did compete in hearts, but South's subsequent strong bidding inspired North to put him in 6♣.

South ruffed West's ♡K opening lead and drew trump, throwing the ♠3 on the third. Visions of overtricks danced in his head:, he counted 14 tricks via a winning diamond finesse, but only 13 if it lost. He led the ♢2 to the ♢K and then the ♢4 towards his ♢AJ.

When East followed with the ♢4---oops, there can't be two fours of diamonds, that was the four of *hearts*---South could not recover. Het lost a diamond and a heart. Down one.

"Fourteen tricks turned to eleven," sighed South. "It could only happen to me." "Yes, only to you, as I'd have settled for twelve," groaned North.

How could you have locked up twelve tricks?

Were West to show out on the ♢2, you'd win the ♢K and take the proven finesse. But when he follows with the ♢3, cover gently with dummy's ♢4 and cry "Deep finesse!"

East will win the ♢9, but you'll win his spade shift in hand, play the ♢A and then the ♢J to dummy's ♢K. Ruff a diamond and cross to dummy's ♠K to discard your last spade on dummy's fifth diamond.

DEAL 5. POSTPONEMENT

```
              ♠ K Q J 10 9 8
              ♡ K 4 3
              ◊ 10 2
              ♣ A 5
♠ 4 3 2                        ♠ 7 6
♡ J 9 8 5                      ♡ Q 10 6
◊ Q J 9 4                      ◊ K 7 6 5
♣ J 3                          ♣ Q 10 8 7
              ♠ A 5
              ♡ A 7 2
              ◊ A 8 3
              ♣ K 9 6 4 2
```

North transferred to spades in response to South's strong 1NT opening, then invited 6♠ while showing six or seven spades and denying shortness in their fancy partnership methods. South liked his prime values for slam purposes, so he accepted.

West led the ◊Q to South's ◊A. South recognized the deal type: a "draw trump and set up a long suit" deal. That's what he did ... in that order, *trumps first*. Then, ♣A, ♣K and club ruff. Back to his hand with the ♡A, his only remaining entry, to lead a fourth club.

However, East had kept his clubs, so when declarer discarded dummy's last diamond on the ♣9, East won the ♣Q and exited with the ◊K.

South ruffed in dummy, but with no hand entry to cash his fifth club, he lost a heart in the end. Down one.

Could South have manufactured the extra hand entry he needed?

No, but he could have conserved the entries he did have. By drawing only one trump with the ♠K, he could start clubs promptly: ♣A, ♣K, club ruff, and back to his ♠A to ruff another club in dummy.

Then he'd still have the ♡A as a hand entry to cash a long club for the twelfth trick he needed.

DEAL 6. SERENDIPITY

```
                    ♠ J 8
                    ♡ K 10 6
                    ◊ 9 8 5 3 2
                    ♣ K 8 6
   ♠ K Q 10 7 5                      ♠ 9 6 4 3
   ♡ 3 2                             ♡ 7 5
   ◊ A J                             ◊ K Q 10 6
   ♣ J 10 7 5                        ♣ Q 9 2
                    ♠ A 2
                    ♡ A Q J 9 8 4
                    ◊ 7 4
                    ♣ A 4 3
```

Favorable vulnerability let South buy the contract for 4♡ despite West's 1♠ overcall and East's 2♠ raise.

Declarer won the ♠K opening lead with the ♠A, drew trump with the ♡Q and ♡J, and exited in spades, hoping for a ruff-sluff. Not to be. West won the ♠Q and found the easy ♣J shift. The defense took two diamond tricks and a club at the end. Down one. Not much of an effort.

"Why did you give up?" asked North.

Do you see any alternative to surrender?

Where there's a long suit, there's hope. Dummy's diamonds provide that hope here, but you must preserve the entries you need to establish and cash a long diamond. You have nothing to lose by starting promptly. Lead the ◊7 to Trick 2. West will win and cash the ♠Q, then lead the ♣J.

Win the ♣A to lead another diamond. West will win and continue clubs. Win dummy's ♣K and ruff a diamond high, ♡Q and low to dummy's ♡10, then ruff another diamond high. A third trump to dummy's ♡10 will let you pitch your remaining club on dummy's fifth diamond and you'll still have a trump left for your tenth trick.

DEAL 7. NO FREE LUNCH

$$\spadesuit\ Q\ 4$$
$$\heartsuit\ K\ J\ 10$$
$$\diamond\ 7\ 2$$
$$\clubsuit\ A\ K\ J\ 8\ 6\ 3$$

♠ 7 6 3   ♠ 8 5
♡ Q 8 5 3 2   ♡ 9 7 6
◊ A Q 3   ◊ 10 9 8 4
♣ 7 5   ♣ Q 10 9 2

$$\spadesuit\ A\ K\ J\ 10\ 9\ 2$$
$$\heartsuit\ A\ 4$$
$$\diamond\ K\ J\ 6\ 5$$
$$\clubsuit\ 4$$

After a game-forcing 2♣ response to 1♠ and eventual tertiary support for spades, South invoked Roman Keycard Blackwood to reach a good but problematic 6♠.

West led the ♡3. South turned to his RHK (Right-Hand Kibitzer) and whispered in her left ear, "Free finesse!"

Dummy's ♡10 won Trick 1. Declarer drew trump and cashed the ♡A. He led to dummy's ♣A and threw his two low diamonds on dummy's two kings. Then he led dummy's ◊2 and tried to guess diamonds. When his ◊J lost to West's ◊Q, he turned to his LHK and whispered in her right ear, "Why do I always misguess aces or queens?" Then West cashed the ◊A.

"You didn't misguess, sweetheart," said South's LHK as she handed him a BLT sandwich. "I had Gertie make this for you. No mayo, right?"

"Who said 'There's no such thing as a free lunch,'?" said his RHK consolingly.

Down one. Any idea how South could have made 6♠? And what's that about a free lunch?

The extra heart trick wasn't free. South paid double for it. He lost the two long club tricks he could have established by keeping his precious ♡4 as an entry to ruff out and reach dummy's long clubs.

DEAL 8. DUCKING TO PRESERVE AN ENTRY

```
                    ♠ 9 8 4
                    ♡ J 5
                    ◊ A 7 3
                    ♣ K 8 7 4 2
     ♠ Q 10 5                          ♠ J 3
     ♡ K Q 10 8                        ♡ 9 7 4 3
     ◊ Q 8 6 2                         ◊ K 10 4
     ♣ 9 6                             ♣ Q J 10 5
                    ♠ A K 7 6 2
                    ♡ A 6 2
                    ◊ J 9 5
                    ♣ A 3
```

South crawled to an iffy 4♠ game on an uncontested auction. He won West's ♡K opening lead with the ♡A and cashed both top trumps. Then he took the ♣A and ♣K, and led a third club.

"Please don't show out," he begged East.

"Anything to oblige," she answered, following with the ♣J.

South ruffed and begged West, "Please don't overruff."

"Wouldn't dream of it," said West smiling her most seductive smile as she discarded the ◊2. When South led the ♡2 to try to reach dummy with a heart ruff, West won the ♡Q, cashed the ♠Q and tapped declarer with the ♡10. Declarer fell two tricks short, taking only four trumps, two clubs and two red aces.

"Tough luck," said North. "I was an entry short. Maybe I should have dropped you in three spades."

Was North right?

Not necessarily. A better declarer ducks Trick 1, thus ensuring a third-round heart ruff as a vital extra dummy entry, and limps home with ten tricks by playing to set up dummy's fifth club as before.

DEAL 9. SAVE THAT ENTRY

```
                      ♠ Q 5
                      ♡ A Q 4
                      ◇ J 7 2
                      ♣ A 9 6 3 2
     ♠ 3 2                              ♠ 6 4
     ♡ J 9 8 6 3                        ♡ K 10 7
     ◇ K 8 5 3                          ◇ Q 9 6 4
     ♣ 7 4                              ♣ Q J 10 8
                      ♠ A K J 10 9 8 7
                      ♡ 5 2
                      ◇ A 10
                      ♣ K 5
```

After a 2♠ jump-shift and an eventual Roman Keycard Blackwood 4NT, South landed in an iffy 6♠ that seemed to depend on a heart finesse. West put declarer to an immediate test with his fancy "third from even, low from odd" ♡3 opening lead.

Declarer played dummy's ♡Q, perhaps too quickly. East won and returned the ♡10 to drive out the ♡A. With clubs 4-2, declarer was now one entry shy of establishing and using the fifth club. Down one.

Do you see how to overcome dummy's entry shortage?

The heart finesse can wait. Just play low from both hands at Trick 1. East can win with the ♡10 if he dares, but he cannot return a heart. Dummy remains with enough entries (♠Q and ♡A) to set up and use the fifth club to discard his diamond loser.

Declarer makes 6♠, losing only one heart.

Note that after an old-fashioned "fourth highest" ♡6 opening lead, South must guess whether to play East for the missing ♡3 and finesse the ♡Q.

But after a "top of internal sequence" ♡9 lead (best only when the higher honor is the ♡J specifically) ducked in dummy, a courageous East could duck and beat the slam.

DEAL 10. PRETTY GOOD ODDS

                          ♠ 8 4
                          ♡ A K 6 4 2
                          ◊ 10 9 3
                          ♣ 9 8 4
    ♠ K 7 3 2   ♠ 9 6 5
    ♡ J 9 7 5   ♡ Q 10 8 3
    ◊ 8   ◊ 7 4
    ♣ Q J 10 6   ♣ 7 5 3 2
                          ♠ A Q J 10
                          ♡ void
                          ◊ A K Q J 6 5 2
                          ♣ A K

North and South were playing "Control Responses" to their Omnibus 2♣ openings. We don't favor them, but some astute experts swear by them.

North's 2♡ response showed an ace and a king (2NT would show three kings). South bid a natural 3◊ and North raised to 4◊. North answered South's 4♠ cue bid with 5♡ to show which ace, and his 6♣ cue bid with 6♡ to show which king. Unable to retreat to 6◊, South gambled 7◊ hoping North had the ◊J and the ♡Q.

Sitting with the ♠K, West couldn't suppress a grin as he led the ♣Q. Declarer won, crossed to dummy in trumps, discarded the ♠10 and ♠J on dummy's top hearts, and ruffed a heart high.

He crossed in trumps again, and ruffed another heart high. If hearts split 4-4, dummy's ♡6 was high. Else he could try the spade finesse.

Did South cross to dummy's last trump to discard the ♠Q on dummy's ♡6? What's that? He couldn't get there?

Did he lead his ◊2 to an earlier trick? Pity! When the ♠K didn't fall under his ♠A, he was down one.

We hope you wouldn't have squandered the ◊2, else we'll have to revoke your membership in Deuce Lovers Anonymous.

DEAL 11. WHICH ROAD TO TAKE?

```
                    ♠ A Q 3
                    ♡ 8 6
                    ◊ A 10 7 6 4 2
                    ♣ 6 5
♠ 9 8                                   ♠ 7 5 2
♡ K 9 7 5                               ♡ Q 10 4 3
◊ K Q 3                                 ◊ J 9
♣ Q J 10 8                              ♣ A 7 3 2
                    ♠ K J 10 6 4
                    ♡ A J 2
                    ◊ 8 5
                    ♣ K 9 4
```

Favorable vulnerability induced West to make a shaded takeout double over South's garden-variety 1♠ opening and East to jump to 3♡ over North's strength-showing redouble in a vain effort to impede further bidding by North and South. The perverse effect was to prod North to jump to 4♠ when 3♡ came round to him, as a mere 3♠ would not convey the strength of his three-card support.

West led the ♣Q. Perceiving the danger of two ruffs in dummy, East won the ♣A and shifted to the ♠2. South won in dummy and led a crafty low heart to his ♡J, but West won and led another spade.

Five spade tricks, three outside winners and only one ruff in diamond meant only nine tricks for declarer, who glared at East and cried "Curse you, Danny!"

How would you have coped with that nasty defender?

Taking two ruffs in dummy is merely Plan B. Once East thwarts it, try Plan A, setting up dummy's long suit. Win the trump switch in dummy and duck a diamond. The defenders can do no better than lead a second trump.

Win in hand, lead a diamond to the ace and ruff a diamond high. Cross to dummy's remaining trump honor to draw the last trump and run diamonds. With both diamonds and spades 3-2, you'll take 11 tricks.

Then, instead of cursing the poor soul, you can smile and say, "Thank you, Danny, for the overtrick. That's the nicest gift I've received since my bar-mitzvah."

DEAL 12. TIMING THE USE OF ENTRIES

```
              ♠ A 8 5 4 2
              ♡ K 10 4
              ◊ A 8
              ♣ 9 6 5
♠ Q 6                        ♠ K J 10 7
♡ 7 5 3                      ♡ 9
◊ K Q 10 2                   ◊ 9 7 6 5 4
♣ Q 8 4 2                    ♣ K 10 7
              ♠ 9 3
              ♡ A Q J 8 6 2
              ◊ J 3
              ♣ A J 3
```

After a routine 1♡-1♠; 2♡-4♡ auction, West led an equally routine ◊ K.

South recognized a "second suit deal" and played ◊A, ♠A and ♠2. East rose with the ♠K to return the ◊5. West won the ◊Q and returned a trump, taking away one of declarer's entries. As we will see in a later chapter, the best defense on a second suit deal is usually to attack dummy's entries.

Declarer won the trump return in dummy and ruffed a spade high. But with spades 4-2, dummy was an entry short. Declarer could establish dummy's last spade, but not reach it. He lost one spade, one diamond and two clubs. Down one.

How would you have timed the play?

By ducking a spade without taking the ♠A first. East can still win the ♠K and return a diamond to West, who can shift to a trump. Now you can win in hand and lead your remaining spade to dummy's ♠A, which serves not only as a trick but as an entry to ruff a spade high.

Dummy's two heart honors remain as the entries you need to ruff another spade high and return to dummy while drawing the defenders' last trump. Then dummy's fifth spade becomes your tenth trick.

The key play? Saving an ace for the time when it serves not only as a trick but also as an entry. You don't have to cash winners immediately.

DEAL 13. KEEP 'EM COMING

```
              ♠ K Q J 10 9
              ♡ 10 6 5
              ◊ 10 5 2
              ♣ 7 4
♠ A 7 6 3                        ♠ 8 5 4
♡ 8 7 3                          ♡ 4
◊ J 8                            ◊ K 9 7 4 3
♣ K 10 8 2                       ♣ J 9 5 3
              ♠ 2
              ♡ A K Q J 9 2
              ◊ A Q 6
              ♣ A Q 6
```

After South opened an Omnibus 2♣, North did well to "wait" with a neutral 2◊ response. Apparently, the North-South methods did not include the popular "natural positive" 2♠ response that would have shut out South's 2♡ rebid. This sensible treatment allowed North to bid a natural positive 2♠ next turn, after which South bid 3♡ showing a sixth heart.

When North then raised to 4♡, South gambled 6♡, probably expecting a lead in a minor to give him an extra trick.

Not today! West led a passive ♡3. South won, finished trumps in two more rounds and led his spade. East had taken the opportunity to discard spades, giving count as he did. West might have risen with the ♠A, but not trusting East's discards entirely, he ducked.

South led another spade from dummy, on which East discarded an encouraging ◊7. West's ◊J shift gave South two diamond tricks to go with six hearts and one trick in each black suit, but that was only 10, so 6♡ failed by two.

Can you come to 12 tricks?

Yes, if you stop to count them before playing to Trick 1: six hearts, two side aces, and four spades. Fortunately, dummy's golden ♡10 provides the entry you need to reach dummy's spades, provided you preserve it.

So after East follows to the first heart, cash only one more. Then start spades promptly while the precious ♡10 is still in dummy.

14

DEAL 14. NEED AN ENTRY? RUFF YOUR WINNER

```
                        ♠ 3
                        ♡ A J 9 8 7 5 3
                        ◊ 3
                        ♣ A K 4 2
        ♠ 6                             ♠ 8 7 4 2
        ♡ K 10 6 4                      ♡ Q
        ◊ J 10 9 6 5                    ◊ K 8 7 4 2
        ♣ Q 7 5                         ♣ J 9 6
                        ♠ A K Q J 10 9 5
                        ♡ 2
                        ◊ A Q
                        ♣ 10 8 3
```

Eddie Kantar invented a 3NT opening that shows a strong preempt in an undisclosed solid major while denying an outside ace, but North and South were playing Danny's version, in which it promised 8 or 8½ winners and usually included an outside ace.

North responded 4◊, asking South to bid his major, then invoked Roman Keycard Blackwood, confirmed that no key was missing, and gambled 7♠ hoping that the hearts would come home.

West led a friendly ◊J to South's ◊Q, giving him a "free finesse" he might not have dared to take on his own. South hummed a few bars of the early Beatles song "Thank You, Girl" and drew trump. Then he started dummy's hearts: ♡A, heart ruff ...

Oops, it was a diamond, not a heart, that East played on the second round. South changed his tune to Elvis Presley's "Little Sister" ... to no avail. He ruffed, crossed to dummy's clubs twice to ruff the hearts good, and cashed the ◊A, but all he could hum was "Heartbreak Hotel." He had no entry to those long hearts and no parking place for his third club.

Could you have overcome the unfriendly 4-1 heart split?

Yes, with a little more thought at Trick 1. Start hearts early, ♡A and ruff a heart, ruff the redundant ◊A with dummy's lone trump ... and now you have entries aplenty to set up dummy's hearts, draw trump and cash them.

DEAL 15. SAVING AN ENTRY

♠ A K 10 9 4
♡ J 9
◊ K Q 9 8
♣ J 7

♠ Q J 8 2   ♠ 6 5
♡ A 10 6 4   ♡ K Q 3 2
◊ 6 5   ◊ 7
♣ Q 8 5   ♣ K 10 9 6 4 3

♠ 7 3
♡ 8 7 5
◊ A J 10 4 3 2
♣ A 2

South opened a hefty Weak 2◊. North, put him in a skinny 5◊ after he showed a club "feature" and a maximum.

West led the ◊5, and declarer drew the last trump at Trick 2. Then he cashed both of dummy's top spades and ruffed a spade. Needing another entry to ruff out the last spade, he crossed dummy's third trump.

After ruffing another spade, he knew dummy's fifth spade was high, but he realized he needed to keep a trump in dummy to a heart. So now he led a heart. East won, but instead of continuing hearts he shifted smartly to clubs.

Alas, South couldn't lead his last trump to dummy to cash the long without losing two hearts and one club in the end. Down one.

Mistimed? Unlucky? Overbid?

Yes, no and maybe. Definitely mistimed. Declarer needed trump entries to ruff out the spades in time. So, starting at Trick 2, two top spades and a spade ruff. A second trump to dummy, and a second spade ruff.

Now declarer can reach dummy with a third trump to discard the ♣2 on the fifth spade, then sit back and lose two hearts while a trump remains in dummy to ruff the third heart and a trump remains in hand to ruff a club.

DEAL 16. MAKING DO

```
              ♠ A K 6 5 2
              ♡ 9 6
              ◇ A J 5
              ♣ 9 6 3
♠ Q J 9 7                        ♠ 10 3
♡ 10 5 4                         ♡ 8
◇ 9 6                            ◇ Q 10 8 4
♣ 10 7 4 2                       ♣ A K Q J 8 5
              ♠ 8 4
              ♡ A K Q J 7 3 2
              ◇ K 7 3 2
              ♣ void
```

South jump-rebid his hearts after East entered with 2♣. He didn't know whether North intended 4◇ next as natural bid or a cue-bid seeking slam, but he didn't care. Either way, his hand was worth a shot at 6♡, so he bid it forthwith.

South ruffed the opening lead and drew trump. He cashed dummy's two top spades and ruffed a third. When spades split 4-2, declarer needed two entries to dummy. He saw how he might get them: via a diamond finesse.

Alas, East not only won the ◇Q but had a second diamond stopper, and the seemingly sound slam failed. One entry short!

Do you see how to make do with the one outside entry to dummy's spades that you had?

You don't need a second entry if you duck a spade first. West can win the first spade and shift to diamonds, but now you can win in hand and then take two top spades, pitching a diamond, and ruff one.

The ◇A will be the one entry you need to pitch a second diamond on dummy's fifth spade.

DEAL 17. FIGHTING CHANCE

```
                    ♠ Q J 8 6 3
                    ♡ K 10 3
                    ◊ J 9 3
                    ♣ Q J
    ♠ 10 9 2                           ♠ A K 7 5 4
    ♡ 6 4                              ♡ 5
    ◊ Q 8 7 5                          ◊ A K 10
    ♣ A 9 6 5                          ♣ 8 7 4 2
                    ♠ void
                    ♡ A Q J 9 8 7 2
                    ◊ 6 4 2
                    ♣ K 10 3
```

East opened 1♠ vulnerable and South preempted with a non-vul 4♡ before his opponents could get into trouble in spades. West led the ♠ 10.

Declarer had four quick losers but West's ♠10 opening lead gave him a chance. He covered with dummy's ♠J and ruffed East's ♠K.

He led to dummy's ♡10 and continued the ♠Q, ruffing off East's ♠A while noting that the ♠9 didn't fall. He led to dummy's ♡K and ruffed dummy's ♠3. This time West's ♠9 did fall, so dummy's ♠8 became high.

How did South reach dummy to discard a diamond on the ♠8?

Aw, don't tell us he had squandered his precious ♡2 on one of the spade ruffs he took?

That's not what he told Jim, his teammate at the other table in a regional team championship when they compared scores. He blamed West, saying she led the ◊5 and the defenders took the first four tricks in diamonds and clubs.

Did he think Jim would actually believe him?

DEAL 18. THE DEVIL GIVES ANOTHER MULLIGAN

```
                    ♠ K J
                    ♡ A K 9
                    ◇ J 8 5 3 2
                    ♣ K Q 7              the Devil
        ♠ 9 8 7 5 4 2                    ♠ A 10 6 3
        ♡ Q 10 5 3 2                     ♡ J 6
        ◇ 9                              ◇ Q 10 7 6
        ♣ 5                              ♣ 6 4 3
                    ♠ Q
                    ♡ 8 7 4
                    ◇ A K 4
                    ♣ A J 10 9 8 2
```

South responded to North's 16-18 high-card-point 1NT opening with an old-fashioned strong 3♣ jump, and leaped to 6♣ over North's 3♡ cue bid.

West led the ♠9. The Devil won the ♠A and returned the ♠3. South discarded his heart loser and cashed his winners. The Devil kept his diamonds and took the last trick.

"May I have a mulligan, Mr. Devil, please?" pleaded South.

"It's Mister Mephistopheles to you. But if you mess up again, I'm keeping your soul," he replied.

This time South discarded his diamond loser at Trick 2. He drew trumps and cashed the ♣AK. When West discarded, declarer lacked the entries to set up the diamonds. Down one again.

"You've just used your last mulligan," said the Devil. "Report at 6:66 tomorrow morning to start shoveling sulfur."

What would you do differently to beat the Devil?

Before leading to dummy's third trump, unblock the ◇AK. Now you won't be one dummy entry short. Poor Mr. Mephistopheles will slink away crying "Curses, foiled again!" without seizing your soul. Who the hell does he think he is anyway, Dr. Sivana?

19

DEAL 19. A CHANGE OF PLANS

```
              ♠ Q 6 5 4 3 2
              ♡ A K 7
              ◊ K 7 3
              ♣ 9
    ♠ K 9                       ♠ A J 10 7
    ♡ Q 9 4 3                   ♡ J 10 6 5
    ◊ 6 5 2                     ◊ 4
    ♣ K Q 10 2                  ♣ J 8 6 5
              ♠ 8
              ♡ 8 2
              ◊ A Q J 10 9 8
              ♣ A 7 4 3
```

Eschewing the 3NT they may have reached at matchpoints, and liking their good diamonds and good controls, North and South bid to a slightly pushy 6◊.

West led the ♣ K. South thanked his lucky stars not to have received the trump lead that would have foiled his plan to ruff three clubs in dummy. Then he embarked upon that plan: ♣A, club ruff, ♡AK, heart ruff, club ruff---

Oops, stuck in Lodi---er, the dummy---again, with no train leaving the station until tomorrow to get back home for a third club ruff. Declarer called for a spade taxi, but East rose with the ♠A to shift to a ruff-killing trump. A club loser meant down one.

Should this wreck your faith in the maxim "Six diamonds always makes?"

Lovely maxim, but it can't be true. Contracts don't make themselves, declarers have to make them. South can make this one with a "fork" akin to the better-known Morton's Fork. Prepare the extra hand entry you need by ducking a spade at Trick 2. If a defender tries to thwart your crossruff with a trump shift, take the other fork in the road.

Win in dummy, spade ruff. Club ruff, another spade ruff. A second club ruff and a third spade ruff. Now draw the last trump pitching the ♡7 from dummy and take the rest with dummy's ♡AK and two long spades.

DEAL 20. TWO HONORS ON ONE TRICK

      ♠ void
      ♡ J
      ◊ A K 9 8 6 2
      ♣ A Q 9 7 6 4

♠ K 9   ♠ A Q 10 8 3 2
♡ K Q 9 8 7 6 5 3   ♡ 4 2
◊ void   ◊ Q J 7 5 4
♣ 10 8 5   ♣ void

      ♠ J 7 6 5 4
      ♡ A 10
      ◊ 10 3
      ♣ K J 3 2

West opened 4♡ on favorable vulnerability. Few know how to handle opposing 4♠ preempts, but most know to overcall 4NT with strong minor two-suiters; that's what North did. South gambled 6♣ courageously in reply.

West led the ♡ K against 6♣. South won the ♡A and drew trump with the ♣A, ♣Q and ♣K. He led the ◊10 and won dummy's ◊K when West showed out.

He cashed dummy's ◊A and tried to slip the ◊9 past East, ruffing off East's ◊J when East covered. He ruffed a spade in dummy and drove out East's ◊Q with dummy's ◊8. Alas, East won the setting trick with the ◊7.

Could you survive the brutal 5-0 diamond split to make 6♣?

Yes. It's seldom right to play two honors on one trick. When West fails to follow to the ◊10, play dummy's deuce. East will win with one of his diamond honors, but then a ruffing finesse against the other will see you home.

DEAL 21. DEAD GIVEAWAY

                     ♠ K 9 5
                     ♡ Q 2
                     ◊ 10 7 4
                     ♣ A Q 8 4 3

    ♠ 4   ♠ Q 8 2
    ♡ A K 9 8 5 3   ♡ J 10 4
    ◊ J 8 3   ◊ K Q 9 5
    ♣ K 10 2   ♣ J 9 4

                     ♠ A J 10 7 6 3
                     ♡ 7 6
                     ◊ A 6 2
                     ♣ 7 6

West's 2♡ opening may be some players' idea of a Weak Two-Bid on unfavorable vulnerability, but it's not ours. West's hand is easily worth a 1♡ opening. Don't get Danny started on the atrocities committed under the name of Weak Twos. He loves Weak 2♡ and 2♠ Bids, but only when used with discipline.

Here the effect of West's atrocity was to elicit an obstructive 3♡ raise from East and goad South into a loose 3♠ overcall that North raised to 4♠. After cashing both top hearts, West shifted to the ◊3. East's ◊9 drove out South's ◊A.

Knowing he needed some luck, he played for West to have king-third in clubs. Low to dummy's ♣Q, ♣A, club ruff and yes! West's ♣K came tumbling down. Needing to be able to draw trumps ending in dummy, he cashed the ♠A and led a low spade toward dummy.

Oops, West showed out. East ruffed the next club with the ♠Q and cashed the ◊K. Down one. Any better ideas?

Yes. Having shown up with ♡AKxxxx and a guarded ♣K, West won't have the ♠Q. So after winning dummy's ♣Q, finesse East for the ♠Q. Then ♣A and a club ruff, ♠A and low to dummy's ♠K, and run clubs for 11 tricks.

DEAL 22. READ ANY GOOD BOOKS LATELY?

```
                    ♠ Q 6
                    ♡ K 9 2
                    ◇ A 8 7 5 2
                    ♣ 7 5 3
    ♠ 10 8 7 3                    ♠ J 9 5 4 2
    ♡ 6 4                         ♡ 7 3
    ◇ Q J 9 4                     ◇ K 10
    ♣ J 10 9                      ♣ Q 8 6 4
                    ♠ A K
                    ♡ A Q J 10 8 5
                    ◇ 6 3
                    ♣ A K 2
```

After an Omnibus 2♣ opening, a semi-automatic neutral 2◇ response, a natural 2♡ rebid and a positive 3♡ raise, South and North cue-bid adroitly to reach a good 6♡ slam.

West led a safe ♣J. South won the ♣A, drew trump with the ♡Q and ♡J, and set about setting up dummy's diamonds by ducking one to East's ◇10. Upon winning East's club return, he led to dummy's ◇A and ruffed a diamond.

Unlucky! A 3-3 diamond split would have seen him home, but when West turned up with four diamonds, he needed two dummy entries to ruff dummy's fourth diamond and return to dummy to cash the fifth.

Having only one, South went down one.

"Didn't you read Dr J's and Mr. Spots' book on Entries?" North asked.

How would South have declared if he had?

To cater to a likely 4-2 diamond split, he'd have ducked a diamond early, before drawing trump. That would have preserved both the ♡K and the ♡9 as the dummy entries he needed to set up and cash dummy's fifth diamond for his twelfth trick.

DEAL 23. LOSE YOUR LOSER EARLY

♠ A 9 7 6 3 2
♡ 9 7
◊ K 2
♣ 8 7 2

♠ K 5
♡ 10 6 4 2
◊ Q 10 9 7 5
♣ J 10

♠ Q 10 4
♡ 3
◊ J 6 4 3
♣ Q 9 6 4 3

♠ J 8
♡ A K Q J 8 5
◊ A 8
♣ A K 5

It's standard expert practice to play an Omnibus 2♣ opener's 3♡ and 3♠ jump rebids as setting trumps while requesting specific ace and king replies, but 3♡ works slightly differently from 3♠.

After South's jump 3♡ rebid here, 3♠ would deny an ace but promise at least one king, and North's 3NT rebid showed the ♠A (and denied a second ace). South's "next step" 4♣ rebid asked for specific kings. North bid 4◊ to show the ◊K. That spurred South to gamble 6♡.

West led the ♣J against 6♡. South won the ♣K, drew trump, cashed dummy's ♠A and surrendered a spade. Oops, he now had only the ◊K as a dummy entry to ruff out the spades but no other dummy entry to cash any.

Down one. Pity to spoil a neat auction with sloppy play!

What basic principle did declarer overlook? How should he play?

Lose a trick you can't avoid losing early rather than late. After drawing trump, duck a spade promptly, retaining dummy's ♠A as an entry to ruff out the suit. Dummy's ◊K will remain as an entry to dummy's established spades. If the defenders haven't dislodged your minor-suit aces, discard them on dummy's last two spades. Your kibitzers will get a kick out of that!

Notice how well a diamond lead would have worked for West. Long suit leads by defenders with long trumps often do.

DEAL 24. WE WON'T TELL ANYONE

```
                    ♠ A J 10 6 4
                    ♡ 7 3 2
                    ◇ K J 4
                    ♣ 8 2
      ♠ K 4 3 2                         ♠ Q 9 7 5
      ♡ J 8 5                           ♡ Q 10 9
      ◇ 6 3                             ◇ 7
      ♣ A 10 6 4                        ♣ K J 9 7 3
                    ♠ 8
                    ♡ A K 6
                    ◇ A Q 10 9 8 5 2
                    ♣ Q 5
```

South declared 5◇ when neither he nor his partner had the club stopper needed for the cheaper game in notrump.

West led the ♣ A, the unbid suit, and continued with the ♣4 to East's ♣K. Upon winning the heart shift, South ran all his diamonds hoping one or both defenders would discard badly or be squeezed in the majors.

But West kept a guarded ♡J and East kept a guarded ♠Q. Down one.

How could you find an eleventh trick?

The only legitimate hope is to set up and cash dummy's fifth spade using the ♠A and dummy's three trumps as entries. Lead a spade to dummy and ruff a spade. Then cross to dummy's ◇J, breathing a sigh of relief when both defenders follow.

Ruff another spade, breathing a second sigh of relief when both defenders follow again. Another trump to dummy's ◇K and a third spade ruff fells the defender's last spade honor.

Now cross to dummy's ◇4 to discard the ♡6 on dummy's ♠J.

You still have the ◇2 in your hand, don't you? What, you don't? Don't worry, Willie, we won't tell anyone it was you who butchered the play. But henceforth, we'll buy our steaks at Erich's Prime Meats just up the hill.

25

DEAL 25. PUT IT IN YOUR POCKET

```
                    ♠ A 6 4 3 2
                    ♡ A J 4 3
                    ◊ 7 4
                    ♣ 8 3
    ♠ J 9 8 7                       ♠ K Q 10
    ♡ ----                          ♡ Q
    ◊ Q J 9 8                       ◊ 10 6 5 3 2
    ♣ K 9 7 5 4                     ♣ J 10 6 2
                    ♠ 5
                    ♡ K 10 9 8 7 6 5 2
                    ◊ A K
                    ♣ A Q
```

North judged well to deem his hand a full-fledged limit raise. South's 4♠ jump was Kickback, the brainchild of Jeff Rubens, a superior form of keycard ask following agreement on hearts as trump. With a hand that would other have cue-bid 4♠, Kickback devotees bid 4NT.

North's 5◊ reply assured South of the two missing aces, and South bid 7♡, gambling on finding a thirteenth trick somewhere, perhaps from ◊Qxx or longer, perhaps from a club finesse, perhaps from a club lead.

Against a small slam, a lead from a king might be a killing lead, but against a grand, it would be suicidal, so West wisely led the ◊Q.

South won and counted twelve his tricks. Seeing only three entries to dummy, he drew trump with dummy's ♡A and bet the farm on a club finesse.

Down one. Sure, swift, but sadly premature. Must we repeat? *Reserve a finesse as a last resort when all your other resources fail.*

Look again at the trumps. Do you see a *third* trump entry? Put the priceless ♡2 in your pocket so you don't waste it ruffing.

Then ruff the spades good using the ♠A, ♡A, ♡J and ♡4 as entries. If the spades don't split 4-3, you'll be in dummy at the end to try the club finesse.

DEAL 26. AGAINST THE ODDS

```
                    ♠ 5 4 2
                    ♡ J 4 2
                    ◇ A K 8 7 5
                    ♣ 10 7
♠ Q J 10 7 6                            ♠ 9 3
♡ 3                                     ♡ 10 8 5
◇ 10 4                                  ◇ Q J 9 3
♣ K 8 6 5 2                             ♣ Q 9 4 3
                    ♠ A K 8
                    ♡ A K Q 9 7 6
                    ◇ 6 2
                    ♣ A J
```

You may want to study this deal to learn how to continue after a strong, artificial and forcing 2♣ opening. North "waited" with 2◇. We strongly recommend restricting responses to 2♣ to this and a natural positive 2♡; anything else preempts *opener*. For example, 3◇ consumes a whole extra level of bidding space.

After a 2♡ rebid and positive 3♡ raise, expert opinion is divided about opener's third bid. Would 3♠ show a second suit (e.g. five hearts and four spades) or the ♠A as a cue bid seeking a heart slam?

As this pair played, 3♠ would show neither but announce an unknown second suit, so South bid 3NT to show the ♠A. But in this book the play's the thing, so we'll spare you the details of how North-South reached 6♡.

South won West's ♠Q lead, counted 11 tricks and thought to set up a twelfth in diamonds before drawing trump, as the ♡J was dummy's only outside entry. He cashed the ♡A and dummy's ◇AK, then ruffed a diamond high. Alas, 4-2 diamonds and only one late dummy entry meant down one.

Any way to overcome the not-unlikely 4-2 diamond split?

Yes. Supplement the fancy bidding by some fancy declarer play. You need only three diamond tricks, not four. Duck a diamond early, at Trick 3. Then you'll need only one dummy entry later. The ♡J will do.

DEAL 27. STAYING A STEP AHEAD

```
                    ♠ K Q 6 4 3
                    ♡ 8 4
                    ◊ J 10 8 6
                    ♣ A 3
    ♠ 9 7                              ♠ A J 10 5
    ♡ K Q 6 3                          ♡ 10 9 7 5 2
    ◊ 7 2                              ◊ 3
    ♣ K Q 10 8 7                       ♣ J 6 5
                    ♠ 8 2
                    ♡ A J
                    ◊ A K Q 9 5 4
                    ♣ 9 4 2
```

West, a disciple of the late Marshall Miles whose four-card overcalls are legendary, overcalled 1♡ despite the adverse vulnerability. That, and East's 3♡ jump over North's 1♠ response, had the perverse effect of pushing North-South to an iffy 5◊ instead of a doomed 3NT.

West led a "surprise attack" ♣K. South won dummy's ♣A and saw dummy's spades as his salvation. Hoping West had the ♠A, he entered his hand twice with trumps to lead towards dummy's spade honors. On the first lead, declarer covered West's ♠9 with dummy's ♠K, which won. On the next lead, East captured dummy's ♠Q with the ♠A, saying, "I like girls."

West overtook East's ♣J continuation with the ♣Q to tap dummy with the ♣10. Declarer ruffed a spade but had one dummy entry too few to ruff another spade and return to dummy to cash the fifth spade. He lost a heart, and watched the defenders exchange "high fives" for beating 5◊ one.

Could you have made 5◊?

Yes, by focusing on the target: setting up *one long spade* for a heart discard *in time*. Instead of wasting time and burning entries, lead dummy's ♠Q to Trick 2. You might even say to East, "You like girls? Here's a nice one for you!" He won't even get a look at a count signal from West.

If he ducks, duck a spade next. Now you'll have time and dummy entries enough to both set up and cash a long spade for 11 easy tricks.

DEAL 28. AS FAST AS POSSIBLE

```
              ♠ A J 9 7 6 4
              ♡ J 10 5
              ◊ 8
              ♣ A 10 2
♠ 8 5                          ♠ K Q 10 2
♡ 3                            ♡ A 2
◊ J 10 9                       ◊ K 7 5 4 3 2
♣ K J 8 7 6 5 3                ♣ 4
              ♠ 3
              ♡ K Q 9 8 7 6 4
              ◊ A Q 6
              ♣ Q 9
```

East's "favorable vulnerability" 3♣ opening got by North, but when South jumped to 4♡, admittedly a gamble, North bid 6♡. Before North could comment, "Don't make seven!" East doubled.

East's double steered West away from an "expected" club lead, as it was a "Lightner" double demanding an unusual lead. East didn't care, he just wanted to increase the penalty. He ducked West's ◊J lead and South won the ◊Q.

"First things first," said South as he led the ♡K to drive out East's ♡A. He won East's ♣4 return and started spades. He played ♠A and a spade ruff, low to dummy's ♡10 and another spade ruff, ◊6 ruffed with dummy's last trump, ♠J covered by East's ♠K, and claimed.

"Not so fast," said West. "How do you expect to get back to dummy?"

Oops, no way. A club loser meant down one. "Genius double!" said West. "Without it, I'd lead a club and hand the contract to declarer on a silver platter."

Could 6♡ be made? North quietly hummed the old Otis Redding hit song, "Sittin' on the Dock of the Bay"; what was he humming about?

Otis was "wastin' time"; that's just what South did when he failed to start spades at Trick 2, while dummy still had the ♣A as a vital entry.

DEAL 29. WHAT'S THE CONTRACT?

```
              ♠ 6 4
              ♡ A K Q 5 4
              ◊ Q 8 5
              ♣ Q 9 4
♠ 8 5 2                        ♠ 10 3
♡ 9 6                          ♡ J 10 8 3
◊ J 10 9 4 3                   ◊ K 7 6 2
♣ 10 8 7                       ♣ K J 3
              ♠ A K Q J 9 7
              ♡ 7 2
              ◊ A
              ♣ A 6 5 2
```

Once North opened 1♡, there was no stopping South. South jump-shifted to 2♠ and rebid 3♠ over North's 2NT next. North raised meekly to 4♠, but South persisted with Roman Keycard Blackwood and stopped in 6♠ upon learning that the ♣K was missing.

South won West's ◊J opening lead, drew trump, and played hearts from the top. When East covered dummy's fourth heart, South ruffed and led to dummy's ♣Q. That lost to East's ♣K and a second club loser meant down one.

South slapped his head and exclaimed "Dummkopf!"

"You don't think you should have bid the slam?" asked his kibitzer.

"No," he replied. "I should have bid seven. It's a Five or Seven Deal."

Well, was South really a dummkopf?

Yes, but not for the reason he said. It was not a "Five or Seven Deal" unless he'd bid 7♠. But he was in 6♠, a slam that was a 5-to-1 favorite, and he tried a 2-to-1 line (hearts 3-3 or the ♣K with West) instead.

After drawing trump, duck a heart. If hearts split no worse the 4-2, an easy 12 tricks. And if West has five hearts with one or two minor-suit kings, there may be some small extra chances on a squeeze.

DEAL 30. ELUSIVE ENTRY

$\spadesuit$ A K 9 7 3
$\heartsuit$ 8 7 3
$\diamond$ 10 6 4
$\clubsuit$ Q J

$\spadesuit$ 8 4 $\spadesuit$ Q J 10 6
$\heartsuit$ 6 4 $\heartsuit$ A 5
$\diamond$ K J 7 3 $\diamond$ 8 5 2
$\clubsuit$ K 10 7 5 3 $\clubsuit$ 9 8 6 4

$\spadesuit$ 5 2
$\heartsuit$ K Q J 10 9 2
$\diamond$ A Q 9
$\clubsuit$ A 2

Against 4$\heartsuit$ reached by a straightforward 1$\heartsuit$-1$\spadesuit$; 3$\heartsuit$-4$\heartsuit$ auction, West, fearing to lead up to a strong hand in a suit where declarer might otherwise take a losing finesse, led the $\heartsuit$4.

East took the $\heartsuit$A and shifted to the $\diamond$8. West won the $\diamond$J and exited safely in trump. Then declarer attacked spades by ducking when West gave count with the $\spadesuit$8. Bravo!

East overtook with the $\spadesuit$10 and continued the $\diamond$5. South hopped with the $\diamond$A and took dummy's $\spadesuit$AK to shed his last diamond. When West showed out, declarer took a "last resort" club finesse. That too failed.

"Nice try," said Southwest, declarer's adoring kibitzer. "Taking all your chances." Was she right? Or would you have found an overlooked chance?

No, she was wrong. It all depends on what you played at Trick 1. The actual declarer played the $\heartsuit$2. If you took care to save it, you'd have a claimer even when West shows out on the third spade.

Ruff dummy's fourth spade (high!) and lead the $\heartsuit$2 to dummy's $\heartsuit$8 so you can discard the $\clubsuit$2 on dummy's fifth spade.

DEAL 31. TWO ROADS TO LOCH LOMOND

```
                          ♠ J 7
                          ♡ A K 5 4 2
                          ◇ 7
                          ♣ A K 8 7 6
        ♠ 5 3                              ♠ A 6 2
        ♡ Q 7 3                            ♡ 10 9 8 6
        ◇ A K 10 9 8 5                     ◇ Q
        ♣ Q 10                             ♣ J 9 4 3 2
                          ♠ K Q 10 9 8 4
                          ♡ J
                          ◇ J 6 4 3 2
                          ♣ 5
```

West dealt and opened a marginal 1◇. North jumped to 2NT to show the two lowest unbid suits. South's 3♠ said, "Between clubs and hearts, I prefer spades." With jack-doubleton support and four outside tricks, North bid 4♠.

Playing "A from AKx..." opening leads, West led the ◇ A. Despite East's encouraging ◇Q signal, presumably showing the ◇J and suggesting a continuation, West shifted to the ♠3. East won the ♠A and continued with the ♠2 to destroy dummy's ruffing power.

South guessed to start hearts. He discarded dummy's ♣6 on the third trump, threw the ◇3 on dummy's top hearts, ruffed a heart, took dummy's top clubs to discard the, and ruffed another heart. Having no road back to dummy and ◇J6 still in his hand, he lost two more diamonds. Down one.

Any road to Loch Lomond?

Two roads. The high road: leave dummy's ♣A uncashed and let East hold the fourth heart. He must put dummy in with the ♣A to cash the ♡6.

The low road: Pitch dummy's ♡2 on the third spade. When West's ♣Q10 fall under dummy's ♣AK, take a ruffing club finesse. If East covers, ruff, cross to dummy in hearts, and feed East a club trick.

He must put dummy back in. Five trump tricks, four top tricks elsewhere and an established third club trick get you to Loch Lomond without any bumps in the road.

DEAL 32. A RAY OF HOPE

```
                    ♠ 6 5 4 3 2
                    ♡ Q 10 8
                    ◊ A 3
                    ♣ 7 5 2
    ♠ Q J 10                           ♠ K 9 8 7
    ♡ J 7 5                            ♡ ----
    ◊ 10 9 7 4                         ◊ K Q 8 5 2
    ♣ A 9 6                            ♣ K Q 4 3
                    ♠ A
                    ♡ A K 9 6 4 3 2
                    ◊ J 6
                    ♣ J 10 8
```

South opened 1♡ and North raised to 2♡. South ignored East's take-out double and bid 4♡. West led the ♠ Q, and North boasted "Straight flush!" as he spread the dummy.

Declarer won the ♠A and despaired. Were his minors reversed, he could ruff a third diamond in dummy. He went quietly down one.

Could you see any chance to make 4♡?

Yes, if you look for deal patterns. Threadbare though it is, dummy's spade suit is a second suit. All you need is (sorry, John, Paul, George and Ringo) ... *entries*. Dummy seems one entry short even when spades split 4-3. But there is a ray of hope.

Sometimes your last resort is a first resort. Hey, if you go down, it's only a northern song---er, another undertrick. At Trick 2, finesse dummy's ♡8. When it wins, ruff a spade high, finesse dummy's ♡10, ruff another spade high and lead low to dummy's ♡Q drawing the last trump.

A fourth spade ruff and dummy's ♠6 is high. Cross to dummy's ◊A, discard the ◊J on the ♠6, and you have 10 tricks. Making 4♡.

CHAPTER 2
No Finessing Please

DEAL 33. NO FINESSE; BASIC SECOND SUIT

```
                      ♠ A 5
                      ♡ A Q J
                      ◊ A 7 6 5 4
                      ♣ K J 9
     ♠ Q J 9 3                        ♠ K 7 4 2
     ♡ 10 9 8 7                       ♡ K 6 5 3
     ◊ Q 10 8                         ◊ K J 9 3
     ♣ 4 3                            ♣ 2
                      ♠ 10 8 6
                      ♡ 4 2
                      ◊ 2
                      ♣ A Q 10 8 7 6 5
```

South opened 3♣ and North raised to 6♣. West led the ♠ Q.

Declarer won dummy's ♠A and drew the ♣K and ♣A . Having never met a finesse he didn't like, he led a low to the ♡J. East won and cashed the ♠K.

Down one. Sure, swift, and wrong.

A 50-50 shot! Can you improve upon those odds?

Yes, if you don't hurry to try the finesse but keep it as a back-up play if Plan A, setting up dummy's diamonds, fails. If diamonds split 4-3 and trumps split 2-1, you're home. If not, the heart finesse remains as Plan B.

So, ♠A, ◊A, diamond ruff high. Low trump to dummy, another diamond ruff. Now another trump to dummy draws the last missing trump, and a heart to dummy's ♡A lets you discard your other heart.

You'll surrender a spade next, but ruff your third spade with dummy's last trump.

Twelve tricks, no finesse, thank you.

DEAL 34. WHICH FINESSE? NEITHER; SECOND SUIT

$$\spadesuit \text{A Q}$$
$$\heartsuit \text{K Q 2}$$
$$\diamond \text{8 6 4 3 2}$$
$$\clubsuit \text{8 4 3}$$

♠ J 9 7 5 2   ♠ K 10 6 3
♡ 8   ♡ 9 4 3
◇ K J 10 7   ◇ 9 5
♣ 10 9 6   ♣ A K Q J

$$\spadesuit \text{8 4}$$
$$\heartsuit \text{A J 10 7 6 5}$$
$$\diamond \text{A Q}$$
$$\clubsuit \text{7 5 2}$$

As you can see looking at all four hands, both finesses were working for East and West, who could make 4♠. But they didn't know it, so after East opened 1♣, South was allowed to buy the contract for 3♡.

West led his partner's suit. When North spread the dummy, South said, "With all that stuff you wouldn't put me in four?"

East took three top clubs and shifted to the ◇9. South played the ◇Q. West won the ◇K and shifted to the ♠5. Placing East with the ♠K for his opening bid, South knew that finessing was futile. He won dummy's ♠A, cashed the ♡A and ◇A, and crossed to dummy's ♡Q to ruff a diamond.

But South was a step behind. He crossed to dummy's ♡A to ruff another diamond, but had no way back to dummy to cash the fifth diamond.

Down one. Unlucky, or can you find a better line?

South's line was fine for 4♡, but he was only in 3♡. He could afford one more loser but not two. Strangely, he'd have made 3♡ if he'd had ◇A7. It's a "second suit" deal with entry and timing problems.

So spurn both finesses. Rise ◇A and lead the ◇Q. When West wins and shifts to spades, rise ♠A to ruff out the diamonds. Now you'll set them up in time and have the dummy entry you need to throw a spade on dummy's fifth diamond.

DEAL 35. ARE YOU A FINESSOHOLIC?

```
                        ♠ A J 8 6 4
                        ♡ K 6
                        ◊ A Q 7
                        ♣ Q J 4
        ♠ 9 2                             ♠ Q 10 7 3
        ♡ 8 2                             ♡ 4 3
        ◊ J 9 6 5 3                       ◊ K 10 8
        ♣ K 10 9 5                        ♣ 7 6 3 2
                        ♠ K 5
                        ♡ A Q J 10 9 7 5
                        ◊ 4 2
                        ♣ A 8
```

South reached 6♡ on strong auction that let East double North' 5◊ "1430" reply to South's Roman Keycard 4NT for the lead. West led the ◊5 against 6♡. South turned to East and asked, "Are you conning me?"

"Would little old me do that to you?" asked East sheepishly.
"Oh yes you would!" answered South, inserting dummy's ◊Q.

"Would you like to join Finessoholics Anonymous?" asked West sweetly. "Here's my card."

East won the ◊K and returned the ◊10 to dummy's ◊A. South led to the ♠K, back to dummy's ♠A, and ruffed a spade high. Alas, West discarded a diamond. With East still holding the master spade and only one dummy entry left, South's hopes faded. South thought for a while and led the ♡5.

"Don't tell me you intend to finesse against the eight of trumps too? Let me take you out of your misery," said West as she covered with the ♡8.

Declarer won dummy's ♡K and shot the last arrow from his quiver. When the club finesse failed, he went down one.

Was there a better line?

Yes, cover West's ◊5 with dummy's ◊7. East can win the ◊10 but then he can't dislodge dummy's ◊A, the vital late entry to dummy's long spade.

DEAL 36. WATCH THOSE SPOTS

```
                    ♠ 8 5
                    ♡ Q J 9
                    ◊ K J 7 3
                    ♣ A K 8 7
♠ K J 9 7 4 3                        ♠ 10 6 2
♡ 10 3                               ♡ 8 4
◊ 8 4                                ◊ A Q 10 6 5 2
♣ 10 5 2                             ♣ 6 3
                    ♠ A Q
                    ♡ A K 7 6 5 2
                    ◊ 9
                    ♣ Q J 9 4
```

South opened 1♡ and reached 6♡ despite bold preemption on favorable vulnerability from West in spades and East in diamonds.

West led the ◊8. South ducked to East's ◊10. When East shifted to the ♠2, declarer saw nothing better than to finesse the ♠Q. Down one.

"Bad luck," said West. "On this vulnerability, I might have jumped to two spades even with a jack-high suit."

"Not entirely," said South. "My partner overbid, She might have downgraded her hand with those worthless diamonds in front of the diamond bidder."

Was South right?

Not entirely. When West led the ◊8, dummy's ◊7 was worth its weight in beer. No spade finesse needed. By winning East's spade shift with the ♠A and drawing two rounds of trump ending in dummy, South could take two marked ruffing finesses through East's honors.

East could cover dummy's ◊K with the ◊A and dummy's ◊J with the ◊Q, but then dummy's well-fermented ◊7 would provide a refreshing discard for declarer's ♠Q.

DEAL 37. WHEN EVERYTHING ELSE IS DOOMED

```
                    ♠ Q J 10 5
                    ♡ A 9
                    ◇ 10 7 5 3 2
                    ♣ 5 2
     ♠ 9 7 3                          ♠ void
     ♡ K J 5 2                        ♡ Q 10 7 4
     ◇ A J 9                          ◇ K 8 6 4
     ♣ K J 7                          ♣ 10 9 6 4 3
                    ♠ A K 8 6 4 2
                    ♡ 8 6 3
                    ◇ Q
                    ♣ A Q 8
```

After West opened 1♣ and East responded 1♡, South entered with 1♠. He breezed into 4♠ when West and North raised their partners' majors.

West led the ♠7. Declarer won in dummy, East showing out. Hoping to ruff a heart and club in dummy, South led dummy's ace and another heart. West won and played another irritating trump. Declarer tried the club finesse, but West won and led his last trump.

Very irritating. Down one, taking only eight top tricks and just one ruff in dummy.

"Butting your head against a stone wall," mumbled North.

Why was South's line doomed? What gate could he have opened?

West's failure to lead a red suit suggested that the top honors in diamond and hearts were split. That meant West needed the ♣K for his opening bid. South's only real hope was to try to set up dummy's long diamonds. So start leading them.

Suppose West wins a diamond at Trick 2. Win his trump continuation in dummy and ruff a diamond. Then a heart to the ace and ruff another diamond. When both defenders follow, you are on the road home.

Back to dummy with a third trump, ruff a third diamond in hand, and (finally) a heart ruff puts you back in dummy to cash a long diamond for a tenth trick.

DEAL 38. RECOGNITION

```
              ♠ A 5
              ♡ K 6 5
              ◊ A 6 2
              ♣ 9 8 5 4 2
♠ Q J 10 3                      ♠ 9 8 7 4
♡ Q 9 2                         ♡ 10 8
◊ K 10 8 7                      ◊ J 9 5
♣ 7 6                           ♣ A J 10 3
              ♠ K 6 2
              ♡ A J 7 4 3
              ◊ Q 4 3
              ♣ K Q
```

Good bidding judgment landed South in 4♡ when he rated his hand too weak for his partnership's 15-to-17 HCP notrumps and opened 1♡. North started with a forcing 1NT response and invited game with 3♡ over South's 2◊ rebid.

South carried on to 4♡. He won West's ♠Q with dummy's ♠A, cashed the ♠K and ruffed a spade. He cashed the ♡K and finessed the ♡J, losing to West's ♡Q. He ruffed the next spade and drew the last trump. When the ◊K was off side, he lost two diamonds and the ♣A. Down one.

Unlucky, two finesses losing, but did South have a better line of play?

As the song goes, "It's still the same old story": hand-type recognition. Didn't you read Dr J's book about finesses? Avoid them if you can. Win the ♠K at Trick 1 to preserve dummy's ♠A entry and lead the ♣Q. Yes, it's a "second suit" deal, so work on dummy's five-bagger.

If East shifts to diamonds (continuing spades is no better) after winning the ♣A, trust him not to have the ◊K and disdain a diamond finesse too. Win the ◊A, ♣K, ♡K and ♡A. Ruff a club while the ♠A remains in dummy to ruff another club.

Finally, ruff the last spade in dummy to discard a diamond on the fifth club. West can ruff with his ♡Q any time, but that trick, the ◊K and the ♣A will be the only three tricks for the defenders.

DEAL 39. NO SUIT TOO SMALL

♠ void
♡ A 7 6 3
♢ 6 5 4 3 2
♣ A Q J 10

♠ 10 7 6 3
♡ 10 9
♢ K J 9 8
♣ 9 8 2

♠ Q 8 5 4 2
♡ 2
♢ Q 10 7
♣ K 5 4 3

♠ A K J 9
♡ K Q J 8 5 4
♢ A
♣ 7 6

After North opened 1♢, he raised South's 1♡ response to 2♡. That left him with a little in reserve, so he cooperated by cue-bidding to show the ♣A when South tried for slam. Visualizing as little as ♡Axxx, the ♣A and any king opposite, South bid 7♡.

Trump leads being the norm against grand slams, West led the ♡10. South finished trumps and counted 12 tricks. She cashed both top spades and ruffed the ♠9, hoping the ♠Q would fall. It didn't, so when Plan A failed, she tried Plan B, a club finesse. Down one.

North marked on his private score a note to buy South a copy of Dr J's book on finesses for her birthday next year. Had she missed a Plan C?

No five-card suit in dummy should be ignored, not even a weak one. It's length, not strength. So, ♡K, ♢A, ♡A and ruff a diamond. Cash two top spades throwing clubs and ruff the ♠9.

If the ♠Q falls, the ♠J will provide a third club pitch and a club ruff for a thirteenth trick. When it doesn't, ruff a second diamond. If both defenders show up with three diamonds (as on the actual layout), ruff the ♠J and ruff another diamond, then cross to dummy's ♣A to dump your last club on dummy's fifth diamond.

If diamonds split badly, a club finesse remains as a *Last Resort*.

DEAL 40. AVOIDING THE OVERRUFF

<pre>
                        ♠ A 7 4
                        ♡ K 4
                        ◊ 6 5
                        ♣ A K 9 5 3 2
      ♠ Q 9 5   ♠ J 10 6 3
      ♡ 10 9 5 2   ♡ 8 3
      ◊ K 10 7 2   ◊ J 9 3
      ♣ J 7   ♣ Q 10 8 4
                        ♠ K 8 2
                        ♡ A Q J 7 6
                        ◊ A Q 8 4
                        ♣ 6
</pre>

After South opened 1♡ and rebid 2◊, a difficult auction landed him in an inelegant 6♡ slam. West, with diamond strength behind South, led the ♡2 thinking to prevent diamond ruffs in dummy.

With only 10 top tricks. South tried for two more via a diamond finesse and subsequent diamond ruff in dummy. After the ♡K and a diamond to the ◊Q, West scuttled Plan A, winning the ◊K and continuing with the ♡10.

South tried Plan B, finishing trumps, then two top clubs and a club ruff hoping for a 3-3 split. The Great Shuffler in the Sky scuttled that plan as He usually does, with a 4-2 club split. Declarer came up two tricks short.

"Four or six deal," muttered South, a confirmed Finessoholic.

"Must you take every finesse you see?" moaned North.

Was a Plan C available to avoid any finesse?

Yes. North's *six* clubs can provide *two* extra winners even against a 4-2 split so long as South takes care to avoid getting overruffed on the third round. Win the heart lead in hand and duck a club.

East can win and shift to diamonds. No finesse, please! ◊A, ♡K and ruff a club low. Finish trumps, cross to dummy's ♠A, and claim 12 tricks. A "six or six" deal: two 4-2 splits will do.

DEAL 41. TAKE YOUR TIME

                         ♠ A Q
                         ♡ J 7 4 3 2
                         ◇ A K J 10
                         ♣ 6 5

    ♠ 8 7 2   ♠ 5 4
    ♡ K 10 8 6   ♡ A Q 9
    ◇ 8 7   ◇ 9 6 3
    ♣ K 10 3 2   ♣ J 9 8 7 4

                         ♠ K J 10 9 6 3
                         ♡ 5
                         ◇ Q 5 4 2
                         ♣ A Q

After South opened 1♠, North-South missed the easier-to-make 6◇ slam for which spades provides a fine second suit and stumbled into the easier-to-bid 6♠. Thinking "just to be on the safe side," West led the ♠ 2.

The finessoholic declarer won the opening lead, finished trumps, crossed to the ◇K and couldn't wait to finesse the ♣Q. Down one. Sure, swift, and wrong.

North reached into his left pants pocket and pressed the button on his i-phone he had programmed for that purpose. It prompted Alexa to chirp, "Partner, did you ever meet a finesse you didn't like?" asked North.

"Will Rogers?" asked South.

"No," answered North. "Me. Mr. Rogers wasn't a bridge expert."

How would Mr. Rogers have declared if he were?

Suits split 4-3 more often than kings are on side. Use dummy's five weak hearts as a second suit. ♠A, ♠Q to verify the 3-2 split, duck a heart. East may rise with the ♡A and shift to clubs: refuse to finesse.

Rise with the ♣A. discard dummy's last club on the ♠K drawing West's last trump, and make dummy the master hand. Dummy's ample diamond entries suffice to ruff dummy's fifth heart good and cash it at Trick 13.

DEAL 42. THE SOCIETY SPEAKS

```
                    ♠ A K 8 7 4
                    ♡ A K
                    ◇ K 7
                    ♣ 7 6 5 4
      ♠ 10 5                        ♠ Q J 9 3
      ♡ 10 7 4 3                    ♡ Q 8 6 2
      ◇ Q J 10 9                    ◇ 8 4 3
      ♣ Q 9 2                       ♣ 10 8
                    ♠ 6 2
                    ♡ J 9 5
                    ◇ A 6 5 2
                    ♣ A K J 3
```

We refuse to show the obscene auction in a book that may be picked up accidentally by small children, but somehow South became declarer in a thin 6♣. He won the opening diamond lead in dummy and finessed the ♣J. When it lost to West's ♣Q, he needed spades to split 3-3 to make his slam. As you can see, that didn't happen. Down one.

This deal spurred protests when Frank Stewart reported it in one of his entertaining and instructive newspaper columns. A radicalized fringe group, the Society of Finessers, bombarded Frank with angry letters, some of which a corrupt postal official diverted to Danny's mailbox. We will reprint here only an excerpt from the least offensive of the intercepted letters.

"Dear [expletive deleted]: We protest your disdain for the finesse, an honorable technique that wins half the time---except in your deals."

Frank's not anti-finesse. He opposes them only when he sees a superior alternative. Once he told Danny, "There are some good finesses on both sides." On this deal, he favored cashing both top trumps, keeping two more to ruff out spades.

When clubs split 3-2, as they must for you to have a chance, and spades split 4-2 (about a 48% chance), you'll have time, entries, and trumps enough to set up the fifth spade for your needed twelfth trick. By finessing, you lose that extra 48% chance the substantial fraction of the time that West has a doubleton or tripleton ♣Q.

DEAL 43. AN UNUSUAL DUCK

                    ♠ K J 8 6
                    ♡ 5 3
                    ◊ K Q
                    ♣ 10 9 6 5 3

♠ 10 3   ♠ 0 2
♡ K J 10 9 6 2   ♡ 8 7 4
◊ A J 10 7   ◊ 9 8 6 4 3
♣ Q   ♣ K J 7

                    ♠ A Q 7 5 4
                    ♡ A Q
                    ◊ 5 2
                    ♣ A 8 4 2

West overcalled South's 1♠ opening with 2♡, and North raised delicately to 2♠, then accepted South's 3♣ game try enthusiastically.

West led his singleton ♣Q against 4♠. South won the ♣A promptly and drew trump. As Frank Stewart says, "If you are going to make a poor decision by playing too fast, the first trick is a good time."

When South next led a club, East won and shifted to hearts. The finesse lost, and South still had a diamond and another club to lose. Down one.

Was there a better line of play? What kind of deal is this?

A second-suit deal, yes, but also a "keep the danger hand out" deal. The road to success is to let West, the safe hand, hold Trick 1. West, helpless, can do no better than play the ◊A and then the ◊7.

Now declarer can win Trick 4, draw trump, and play the ♣A and another. By the time East leads a heart through, the clubs are ready to roll. South wins the ♡A and runs them.

No heart finesse needed, thank you.

DEAL 44. COMBINING YOUR CHANCES

                          ♠ J 9 2
                          ♡ 4
                          ◊ A 10 9 7 6
                          ♣ A 7 6 5
       ♠ K 7   ♠ 4
       ♡ Q J 9 2   ♡ 10 8 6 5 3
       ◊ J 5 2   ◊ K Q 8 4
       ♣ K J 9 2   ♣ Q 8 3
                          ♠ A Q 10 8 6 5 3
                          ♡ A K 7
                          ◊ 3
                          ♣ 10 4

An ambitious auction led to an iffy 6♠. All the aces were present, but South had the one king that would do him least good. He turned to his RHK (Right-Hand Kibitzer), fingered the ♡K and griped, "Useless."

South won West's ♡Q with the ♡A, crossed to the ◊A, and let dummy's ♠9 ride for a finesse. West took the ♠K and exited with the ♠7 to dummy's ♠J. South ruffed a diamond in hand and ruffed his ♡7 with dummy's ♠2.

He reentered dummy with the ♣A to ruff another diamond. Wriggle as he might, he had no place to park his remaining club. Down one.

West, a double-dummy expert, said, "I should have led a club." Yes, a club lead would give declarer no chance, but could you make this slam after the normal ♡Q lead?

Those dummy entries are too precious to waste on a trump finesse that may lose, perhaps even to a singleton ♠K. Instead, lay down the ♠A. Only low spades fall beneath it? Don't panic. Work on dummy's diamonds. ◊A, diamond ruff. Heart ruff, another diamond ruff. "Useless" heart king?

Lead him ... straight to the guillotine. Ruff with dummy's last trump, and ruff dummy's fourth diamond. Whether West overruffs or discards, the ♣A is still in dummy as an entry to dummy's fifth diamond for a club discard.

DEAL 45. COMBINING YOUR CHANCES

```
                    ♠ K J 10 5 4
                    ♡ A J
                    ◇ A 8 3 2
                    ♣ 3 2
    ♠ 8 7                           ♠ Q 9 6
    ♡ K 9 7 6 4                     ♡ 10 8 5 3 2
    ◇ 4                             ◇ 7 5
    ♣ Q J 10 8 4                    ♣ K 7 5
                    ♠ A 3 2
                    ♡ Q
                    ◇ K Q J 10 9 6
                    ♣ A 9 6
```

South opened 1◇ and jumped to 3◇ over North's 1♠ response. Now North made a good bid, 3♡. South was happy to give a 3♠ preference, but when North then bid 4◇, he realized that 3♡ might be an advance cue bid and cooperated with a 5♣ cue bid of his own. That was all North needed to put South in the 6◇ slam.

South won West's ♣Q opening lead and drew trump. He played on spades, choosing the best play in the suit, the ♠A followed by a finesse of the ♠J. Down one.

"I had a feeling I should have taken the heart finesse," he moaned. North was not sympathetic.

Which finesse would you have taken and why?

Best is to combine your chances. By playing the longer suit, spades, from the top, you have a chance to drop a short queen. When the ♠Q doesn't fall beneath the ♠K and ♠A, lead the ♡Q and let it ride if not covered.

Did you take care to preserve dummy's ◇A and ◇8? Good, now you have the two dummy entries you need to discard your third spade on dummy's ♡A, then ruff out and cash the rest of dummy's spades.

DEAL 46. PLAYING THE ODDS

♠ A K 6 5
♡ A Q 7 6 5
◊ Q J
♣ 4 3

♠ 10 7   ♠ 4 3
♡ 8 2   ♡ K J 10 9
◊ K 9 5 3 2   ◊ 10 8 6 4
♣ Q J 10 9   ♣ 8 5 2

♠ Q J 9 8 2
♡ 4 3
◊ A 7
♣ A K 7 6

In their partnership methods, North's 2NT response to South's 1♠ opening was a Jacoby Forcing Raise, showing a balanced hand with at least four spades and values for game or more. South's 3NT rebid denied shortness while promising moderate extra strength. North showed the ♡A and extras with a 4♡ cue bid.

South used Roman Keycard Blackwood to confirm that no ace or high trump honor was missing and learn that North held neither red king. That put a grand slam beyond reach, and they stopped in 6♠.

South won West's ♣Q opening lead with the ♣A and drew trump with the ♠A and ♠Q. He tried the heart finesse first. When East captured dummy's ♡Q with the ♡K and shifted to the ◊4, South tried the diamond finesse. It lost too, despite the 3-to-1 odds against both finesses failing.

Could you get better odds?

Yes. Hearts split 3-3 or 4-2 about 84% of the time. Once trumps split 2-2 and the ♡Q loses to the ♡K, you'll do better to bet on hearts splitting than on a 50% diamond finesse.

Win East's diamond shift with the ◊A and lead to dummy's ♡A. When both defenders follow, you can ruff out the hearts to set up a long heart for a diamond discard, using club ruffs for the dummy entries you'll need.

Note that ruffing clubs in dummy early is bad policy when you may need ruffs later for entries.

DEAL 47. RESISTING TEMPTATION

```
                        ♠ K 4 3
                        ♡ A Q 2
                        ◊ 6 4
                        ♣ A 9 5 4 2
        ♠ 8 6                             ♠ 7
        ♡ 8 7 6 5                         ♡ K J 10 9
        ◊ K 10 8 7 2                      ◊ J 9 5 3
        ♣ 10 7                            ♣ Q J 8 3
                        ♠ A Q J 10 9 5 2
                        ♡ 4 3
                        ◊ A Q
                        ♣ K 6
```

South's 2♠ jump shift, North's raise, and their subsequent cue bids of aces and kings landed them in 6♠, but the price of cue-bidding was East's double of North's 4♡ cue bid, guiding West to lead the ♡8.

Declarer finessed dummy's ♡Q, but East won the ♡K and continued the ♡J to drive out dummy's ♡A. Declarer drew trump with the ♠A and ♠Q, then tried to ruff out the clubs.

Had clubs split 3-3, he'd have succeeded. When they split 4-2, he needed to use dummy's carefully-preserved ♠K as an entry to ruff a second club. Alas, dummy had no entry left to cash the fifth club.

Any way to escape that sad fate?

Yes, two ways. One was to duck the ♡8 lead, hoping East would be unable to play lower. That would have worked, as East had no low heart. But after the heart finesse failed and the heart return dislodged dummy's ♡A, declarer could play ♠Q, ♣K, and the ♣A.

Now a club ruffed high, then lead a spade other than the ♠2 to dummy's ♠K, ruff another club high and lead the ♠2 to dummy's ♠4. Cash dummy's fifth heart for a twelfth trick.

Making 6♠ with both kings offside.

DEAL 48. PROTECTING YOUR SECOND SUIT

```
                    ♠ 10 8
                    ♡ A 8 5
                    ◊ A 8 7
                    ♣ A J 5 4 2
     ♠ 6 4 3                      ♠ K Q J 9 7 5
     ♡ J 10 7 6                   ♡ void
     ◊ Q 6 5 3                    ◊ K J 10 9
     ♣ 9 7                        ♣ Q 10 8
                    ♠ A 2
                    ♡ K Q 9 4 3 2
                    ◊ 4 2
                    ♣ K 6 3
```

East's 1♠ overcall did not impede the North-South auction to 4♡.

After winning the spade lead, South drew three rounds of trump ending in hand. Then he cashed the ♣K and lost a finesse to East's ♣Q. East cashed a spade and shifted to the ◊J.

Declarer won dummy's ◊A and tried to cash the ♣A, but West ruffed and led to East's ◊K. Down one.

Ten winners but four losers; how could you handle this?

Keep your winners and entries intact. Preserve dummy's ♣A as a winner and dummy's ◊A as an entry when you'll need it. When West follows to the second club, win dummy's ♣A and surrender the now unavoidable club loser.

Then dummy's fourth club is ready to supply the diamond discard you need while West ruffs helplessly with his trump winner.

It's a variant of a loser-on-loser play.

DEAL 49. NO GUESSES

      ♠ J 10 3
      ♡ J 10 4
      ◊ K J 8 5 2
      ♣ A K

♠ Q 9 4 2　　　　　　　　　♠ A 8 7 6
♡ K 6　　　　　　　　　　　♡ 7 3
◊ 6 4　　　　　　　　　　　◊ Q 10 9
♣ Q J 10 5 3　　　　　　　♣ 9 8 6 2

      ♠ K 5
      ♡ A Q 9 8 5 2
      ◊ A 7 3
      ♣ 7 4

A routine auction put South at the helm in 4♡. After winning dummy's ♣K at Trick 1, he let dummy's ♡J ride, losing to West's ♡K. He won the next club perforce and drew the outstanding trumps with the ♡A. Dreaming of overtricks, he attacked diamonds, taking the ◊A and finessing dummy's ◊J.

Oops, East won the ◊Q and shifted to the ♠6. Here comes the guess: East wouldn't underlead the ♠A, would he? For East, this might be a "Use it or lose it!" situation.

If East were Danny, who is engaged in a six-decade contest with Eddie Kantar to see who can lose the most aces on defense, it would be easy to rise with the ♠K, but the actual East was a well-dressed stranger.

South guessed wrong. Down one.

How would you guess the spades?

Trick question. No need to guess anything. You have three of the top five spades in the combined hands. That's one sure spade trick even if you lose two.

Start spades instead of diamonds. After losing to both the ♠A and ♠Q, you can discard a possible diamond loser on dummy's ♠10.

DEAL 50. NO THANKS

        ♠ A 5 3 2
        ♡ Q J 10 3
        ◊ 9 6 4
        ♣ 4 2

♠ 9   ♠ 7 4
♡ 9 8 7   ♡ K 6 5 2
◊ K J 5 2   ◊ Q 10 7
♣ A Q 8 7 5   ♣ J 10 9 3

        ♠ K Q J 10 8 6
        ♡ A 4
        ◊ A 8 3
        ♣ K 6

What should West lead after an uncontested 1♠-2♠-4♠ auction?

We don't know. A case can be made for an active ◊2 or a passive ♡9 lead. In *The Bridge World*'s "Master Solvers Club," which Danny directs twice yearly, he estimates the chance of any two expert panelists agreeing on a given problem, including opening leads, as less than one in three.

This West stayed passive. She led the ♡9. South played dummy's ♡Q, but East knew to wait for the last of dummy's equals to cover.

South resisted the temptation to thank East for playing low and the stronger temptation to lean over and kiss her. He drew trump ending in dummy to lead towards his ♣K. West won the ♣A and cashed the ♣Q before exiting safely with the ♡8 to South's ♡A. Declarer lost two diamond tricks and his game contract.

How would you have untangled the entries to take 10 tricks?

Think "entries" *before playing to Trick 1*. Say "No Thanks" to the "free"---er, we mean *costly*---heart finesse. Then lean over to kiss West for not finding the diamond lead that could beat you.

Play the ♡3 from dummy at Trick 1, take the ♡A, ♠K and ♠Q, and lead the ♡4 to dummy's ♡10 and East's ♡K. Dummy's ♠A remains as the entry to dummy's ♡QJ, on which your two diamond losers go away. Ten easy tricks.

DEAL 51. READ ANY GOOD BOOKS LATELY?

```
                    ♠ A K J 6
                    ♡ A J 7 5 2
                    ◇ 2
                    ♣ K 8 5
    ♠ 8 7                          ♠ Q 10 4 3
    ♡ K 6 3                        ♡ Q 10 9 4
    ◇ A Q 8 7 6 4                  ◇ 10 9 5 3
    ♣ 10 3                         ♣ 6
                    ♠ 9 5 2
                    ♡ 8
                    ◇ K J
                    ♣ A Q J 9 7 4 2
```

East's obstructive jump raise of West's Weak 2◇ Bid did not deter South from bidding 5♣ in reply to North's takeout double. With pure values and a bit extra, North gambled 6♣.

West 's ◇A opening lead turned South's ◇K into a winner but didn't help declarer much. Neither did West's ♠8 shift. Declarer won the ♠K, drew trump ending in hand and finessed dummy's ♠J. Down one.

"Didn't you read Jim's book on finesses only as a *last resort*?" asked North.

How might he declare if he had?

By setting up dummy's five-card heart suit. Timing is crucial to preserve a late dummy entry. ♠K, ♣A, ♡8 to the ♡A, ruff a heart high, ♣9 to the ♣K, and another heart ruff.

Ruff your ◇K (it's more useful as an entry than a winner) with dummy's last trump, and ruff one more heart. When the last missing heart falls, cross to dummy's ♠K. Discard your last spade on dummy's ♡J and take the rest.

DEAL 52. NOT ANOTHER FINESSE, PARTNER?

```
                        ♠ 8 6
                        ♡ Q J 8 6 2
                        ◊ K 8 6 4 2
                        ♣ 8
        ♠ K 9 3                          ♠ 10 7 5 4 2
        ♡ 7 5                            ♡ 4
        ◊ A 10 5 3                       ◊ Q J 9
        ♣ Q 9 5 3                        ♣ K 10 7 4
                        ♠ A Q J
                        ♡ A K 10 9 3
                        ◊ 7
                        ♣ A J 6 2
```

South opened 1♡ and gambled 6♡ over North's "Weak Freak" 4♡ raise. jumped to 4♡, South bid 6♡. West led the ♡5 to cut down on dummy's ruffing power and avoid blowing a trick by leading something else.

Declarer won, drew the last trump and bet everything on a spade finesse. That bet lost, and South was down quickly.

North marked "1729" on a tiny notepad he kept in a pocket. "Isn't that Ramanujan's Number?" asked West, peering over her shoulder to look.

"Huh?" grumbled North. "It's just the number of slams blown, lifetime, by my partners who took finesses as first resorts instead of last resorts."

How could you have kept him from infringing Ramanujan's patent?

Before betting the house on one play, look for alternatives. You can still finesse spades later if you need to. At Trick 2, lead the ◊7. Without any signal from East, West won't know whether to duck the ◊A if he has it.

But chances are West will win the ◊A and exit in trumps. Win in dummy and ruff out the diamonds. With a 4-3 split and the ◊A on side, you'll be able to discard the ♠J and ♠Q, then crossruff for 12 tricks. You can take a spade finesse as a last resort, but on this deal you won't need to.

DEAL 53. FIRST TRANSFER THE DANGER

```
                          ♠ J 2
                          ♡ J 8 6
                          ◊ K 9 7 4 3
                          ♣ A Q 3
        ♠ Q 9 7 5                          ♠ 6 4 3
        ♡ 10 9 5                           ♡ A K Q 7 4 3
        ◊ J 5                              ◊ 6
        ♣ J 10 9 7                         ♣ K 6 2
                          ♠ A K 10 8
                          ♡ 2
                          ◊ A Q 10 8 2
                          ♣ 8 5 4
```

East braved North's 3◊ limit raise to overcall 3♡, provoking a "sheep for a lamb" 5◊ gamble from South.

West led the ♡10. When declarer played low and East discouraged with the ♡3, West shifted smartly to the ♣J. Desperate, declarer covered with dummy's ♣Q. East won the ♣K and guessed to continue with the ♣6.

Declarer won in dummy, drew trump with the ◊A and ◊K, and desperately let dummy's ♠J ride. West won the ♠Q and cashed the ♣10.

Two failing finesses and down two. What grief! Could you have avoided that grief?

First, take time to think at Trick 1. A club through dummy's tenace is the main menace. West is the danger hand, so cover his ♡10 with dummy's ♡J to force East, the safe hand, to win Trick 1.

First hurdle cleared, as East cannot attack clubs. Ruff East's heart continuation and draw trump ending in dummy. Now you can float the ♠J, not caring if it loses, as then your three spade honors will provide two club discards.

Losing only a heart and a spade and making 5◊.

DEAL 54. BAD LUCK

        ♠ K 5
        ♡ A J 8 3
        ◇ A J 10 8 3
        ♣ 7 3

♠ 6 3 2   ♠ 8 7
♡ 6 2   ♡ Q 10 9 5
◇ 9 7 4 2   ◇ K Q 6
♣ A Q 8 2   ♣ K 10 9 6

        ♠ A Q J 10 9 4
        ♡ K 7 4
        ◇ 5
        ♣ J 5 4

Correctly deeming his hand a bit too strong for a Weak 2♠ Bid, South opened 1♠. He rebid 2♠ over North's 2◇ response, and lacking a club stopper, had nothing better than to bid 3♠ over North's 3♡ rebid.

Unable to diagnose the 4-4 club split, North could do nothing but raise to 4♠, missing the cold (as the cards lay) 3NT game.

Fearing club ruffs in dummy, West led the ♠ 2.

Declarer won the ♠9 and finessed dummy's ♡J. East won the ♡Q and returned the ♠8. Declarer took the ♠A and ♠Q in hand, but when hearts failed to split 3-3, had to lose three clubs in the end. Down one.

"Bad luck," South complained. "The queen of hearts was off side."

"Another finesse," sighed North. "Did you ever refuse one?"

How would you declare after reading Jim's book on finesses?

Reserve the heart finesse as a *last resort*. At Trick 2, lead to dummy's ◇A and ruff a diamond high. Back to dummy's ♠K and ruff another diamond high. The last of the royal couple falls.

Draw the last trump and lead to dummy's ♡A to cash dummy's ◇J10. Take your ♡K. 11 tricks in all, but if you really love complaining you can say: "Bad luck! The queen of hearts didn't fall, else I'd make six."

DEAL 55. ROLLING THE DICE

```
                    ♠ J 9 8 3
                    ♡ Q 7 4
                    ◊ A 7 3
                    ♣ K J 4
    ♠ K 6                          ♠ 5 2
    ♡ K 6 3                        ♡ 9 8 5 2
    ◊ Q J 10 8                     ◊ 9 6 4
    ♣ A 7 6 5                      ♣ 10 8 3 2
                    ♠ A Q 10 7 4
                    ♡ A J 10
                    ◊ K 5 2
                    ♣ Q 9
```

Had South tried 3NT over North's 3♠ limit raise, North would have pass with his flat shape and we'd have a different story to tell, but he didn't.

West led the ◊ Q against South's actual 4♠. Declarer won in dummy and went after trumps. West captured dummy's ♠9 with the ♠K and persisted with the ◊10. Declarer won the ◊K, crossed to dummy's ♠8, and floated the ♡Q, losing a second finesse to West's ♡K. The ◊J and ♣A meant down one in a hurry.

"Bad luck," said South. "A 75% chance, either of two finesses working, failed."

"Too bad you didn't try a 'second suit' play, the 100% chance," wailed North. "I guess you like to gamble."

"Are you ditsy, Mitzi?" said South. "You had no 'second suit.' You were flat."

"Who are you calling 'flat'?" chirped Mitzi. "I have perfect pitch."

Before the argument gets any nastier, let's settle it. We have an epithet for Mitzi, but it's not "Ditsy." Though it wasn't long, Mitzi did have a second suit: clubs.

No need to roll the dice. Win Trick 1 in hand, lead the ♣Q to drive out the ♣A, win the next diamond in dummy, pitch your diamond loser on dummy's third club, take the money and run.

DEAL 56. A BETTER WAY HOME?

```
              ♠ A J 5
              ♡ J 4 2
              ◇ A J
              ♣ A J 5 4 2
♠ 9 4 2                        ♠ 7
♡ K Q 3                        ♡ 8 7 6 5
◇ K 10 8 5 3                   ◇ Q 9 7 4
♣ K 10                         ♣ Q 9 8 6
              ♠ K Q 10 8 6 3
              ♡ A 10 9
              ◇ 6 2
              ♣ 7 3
```

Had North jumped to 4♠ directly over South's Weak 2♠ bid, as some might, a normal ♡K opening lead from West would have made life easy for South. But wary of the skimpy Weak Twos that have become fashionable over the years, North forced with 2NT and South's 3♡ rebid showed a maximum with a heart "feature" [a delightfully vague term]. So when North bid the 4♠ game, West led the ◇5.

Declarer won in dummy, drew trumps, and finessed hearts twice, a 75% chance. Down one.

Unlucky, or was there a better way home?

Both. The chance of a 3-3 or 4-2 club split is a bit better than 75%, though there are hazards in trying for it. To carry out this plan, you need three dummy entries: two to ruff clubs and one to reach dummy's fifth club. The ♣A is one of those entries, so don't burn it too early.

At Trick 2, start clubs by leading low from dummy, a Morton's Pickle Fork. East can't afford to play the ♣K lest he pickle West's ♣Q, and vice versa. West will win and can lead low (nice play!) to East's ◇Q to get a heart shift.

You can duck, but after West wins and shifts to trump, win in hand. Take the ♣A and ruff a club high, cross to the ♠J and ruff another club high, lead to dummy's ♠A and throw a heart on dummy's fifth club.

DEAL 57. DID YOU EVER HAVE TO
MAKE UP YOUR MIND?

♠ A 10 2
♡ A K 8 7 5
◊ J 9 8
♣ 10 2

♠ K Q J 9 8 7
♡ 10 2
◊ 6 5 3
♣ A Q

You open 1♠, rebid 2♠ over partner's 2♡ response, which your partner insists on playing as game-forcing, and bid 4♠ over his 3♠ raise.

West leads the ◊K and continues with the ◊Q and ◊10 to East's ◊A. East puts you to the test with a shift to the ♣5. The ace or the queen? Decide now.

"You're a mean man, Danny Kleinman," said Danny's girlfriend when he posed this problem to her. "Why don't you show me all four hands like your friend Jim does? I know you like the ladies, so I bet you go for the queen, but she's only 50%."

I think I can do better. Up with the ace, and ruff out the hearts, where I only need a 3-3 or 4-2 split to set up dummy's fifth heart for a club pitch."

"Ha!" said Danny. "You don't know how tricky I am." Then he wrote out East's hand on another scrap of paper: ♠5 3 ♡9 ◊A 7 4 2 ♣K 7 6 5 4 3.

"Down two. East ruffs the second heart and cashes the ♣K."

So what did you decide?

Ignore results. Though the wrong play works and the right play fails, you should listen to the girlfriend. A suit splits 3-3 about 36% of the time and 4-2 about 48% of the time. That's a success rate of about 84% for ruffing out a five-card suit missing six cards in it.

Think of these most common splits as legs of a right triangle with a 60% hypotenuse. Even when played by Ingrid Bergman in *The Eternal Triangle*, the hypotenuse is never as long as the sum of the legs.

DEAL 58. IGNORING THE MIRAGE

```
                      ♠ 8 3 2
                      ♡ K 10 3
                      ♢ 8 7 5 4 2
                      ♣ A 3
         ♠ J 9 7 4                      ♠ K Q 10
         ♡ 6 5 4                        ♡ 2
         ♢ K 10                         ♢ J 9 6 3
         ♣ K 8 7 6                      ♣ Q 10 9 4 2
                      ♠ A 6 5
                      ♡ A Q J 9 8 7
                      ♢ A Q
                      ♣ J 5
```

South reached 4♡ via the obvious route. West, who'd been taught misguidedly never to lead from kings, led the ♠4.

Declarer won the ♠A and drew trumps, ending in dummy. He lost a diamond finesse to West's ♢K. The defenders took the next two tricks in spades; West overtook East's ♠10 with the ♠J to lead the thirteenth spade. Declarer ruffed but lost a club trick in the end.

Down one after a 50% play. Do you think you could do better?

Interestingly, if the ♢Q were a diamond, declarer might have done better. What kind of deal is this? Yes, a second-suit deal, not a deal for a finesse. But timing is crucial. Stay a step ahead.

At Trick 2, cash the ♢A and continue with the ♢Q, just as you would if it were a deuce. You have the timing and entries to set up a long diamond. If diamonds are no worse than 4-2, you can discard your club loser.

This is an 84% play. The ♢Q is a mirage.

More interestingly still, a lead away from the ♣K wrecks this plan. Leading from kings is often desirable. Here doing so attacks a vital dummy entry early.

DEAL 59. WHO NEEDS AN ACE

```
              ♠ K 8
              ♡ A 10 6 3 2
              ◊ K 8 6 3 2
              ♣ K
♠ 2                          ♠ Q 7 3
♡ 7 4                        ♡ K 8 5
◊ J 9 7 4                    ◊ Q 10 5
♣ Q J 9 5 4 2                ♣ 10 8 6 3
              ♠ A J 10 9 6 5 4
              ♡ Q J 9
              ◊ A
              ♣ A 7
```

When North eventually showed tertiary spade support, South drove to a good but still hazardous 6♠.

Upon winning West's ♣Q opening lead in dummy, declarer cashed the ♠K and ♠A, hoping the ♠Q would fall. When she didn't, he had only the heart finesse to fall back on.

That too failed. Not his day. Down one. Sad, nice hand.

Was there a better line of play than a heart finesse?

Yes, when dummy has another five-card suit. Can it hurt to try to set up diamonds? Let's see how that can work.

After winning the ♣K at Trick 1, unblock the ◊A. Cross to the ♠K and ruff a diamond. Avoid the finesse if possible. What about a second suit?

Short of dummy entries? Ruff the ♣A in dummy and ruff another diamond. Now play the ♠A and when the ♠Q doesn't fall, feed her a low trump. Ruff East's club return and cross to dummy's ♡A.

Dummy's ◊K8 will provide discards for declarer's remaining hearts.

Was there any better use for the ♣A than to ruff it in dummy?

DEAL 60. ONE HELPS THE OTHER

```
                  ♠ A Q
                  ♡ J 7 4 3 2
                  ◇ A K J 10
                  ♣ 6 5
   ♠ 8 7 2                        ♠ 5 4
   ♡ K 10 8 6                     ♡ A Q 9
   ◇ 8 7                          ◇ 9 6 3
   ♣ K 10 3 2                     ♣ J 9 8 7 4
                  ♠ K J 10 9 6 3
                  ♡ 5
                  ◇ Q 5 4 2
                  ♣ A Q
```

Playing Two-Over-One Game-Forcing, North responded 2♡ to South's 1♠. Perhaps thinking to save bidding space, he bid 2NT over South's 2♠ rebid. South bid 3◇ next, North temporized with 3♠, and South cue-bid 4♣ to show the ♣A. When North answered with a 4◇ cue bid in return, they reached 6♠.

North would have done better to bid 6◇ directly over South's 4♣. Standard bidders could find the superior diamond slam after a natural forcing 3◇ rebid by North.

West led the ♠2. Declarer finished trumps in three rounds and relied on a club finesse. When it failed, down one.

Sure, swift, and wrong. Do you see a better line of play?

Perhaps. The finesse can be held in reserve if not forced earlier. The chance of a 4-3 heart break exceeds the 50% chance of the club finesse, though only by a small margin.

Dummy's diamonds provide the entries you need to try to set up a fifth heart. You might lead a low heart from dummy at Trick 2. East will win.

A good defender will put you to the test by shifting to clubs promptly. Would you pass that test? You'd have to judge whether he would switch to clubs even if he had the ♣K.

DEAL 61. DECLARE OR DEFEND?

```
                    ♠ A 7 6 5 2
                    ♡ 10 2
                    ◇ K 5 3
                    ♣ A 7 3
♠ Q J                               ♠ K 10 9 3
♡ 7 6 4                             ♡ 8 5
◇ J 10 9 8                          ◇ A Q 7 6
♣ Q 8 5 2                           ♣ 10 9 6
                    ♠ 8 4
                    ♡ A K Q J 9 3
                    ◇ 4 2
                    ♣ K J 4
```

After a 1♡-1♠; 2♡ start, North faced a close choice between 2NT and 3♡. He chose 2NT. We wouldn't. Then South faced a close choice between 3NT and 4♡. We wouldn't either, but neither of us is a hand hog.

West led the ◇ J. South ducked this and West's ◇10 continuation. East had the opportunity to overtake the second diamond with the ◇Q and shift to the ♣10 (attacking dummy's entry!), but missed it.

West led a third diamond. Declarer ruffed, drew trump, and relied on a club finesse for his contract. When it lost, an unavoidable spade loser put him down one.

Was South's the best plan? How would you have declared 4♡?

How about trying to set up dummy's spades in dummy instead of relying on a 50% finesse? At Trick 4, duck a spade, preserving dummy's ♠A as an entry. East can overtake West's honor with the ♠K and shift to clubs,

Win the ♣K and ruff out the spades, using the ♡10 and (after finishing trumps) the ♣A as entries. Away goes your club loser on dummy's fifth spade.

CHAPTER 3
No Ruffing Please

DEAL 62. THE COMPULSIVE RUFFING SYNDROME

```
                        ♠ 6 5 3
                        ♡ K Q 5 4
                        ◇ void
                        ♣ Q J 8 6 5 4
    ♠ Q J 8 7 2                        ♠ A K 9
    ♡ 10 9 7                           ♡ 3
    ◇ 10 9 7                           ◇ A K J 8 6 5
    ♣ 7 2                              ♣ K 9 3
                        ♠ 10 4
                        ♡ A J 8 6 2
                        ◇ Q 4 3 2
                        ♣ A 10
```

East opened 1◇. After South overcalled 1♡, North jumped to 4♡. Should East pass or double? At this level, though doubles are best still played for takeout, they'll often be passed by a partner who has nothing better to do. A tough decision for East whether to double, and if he does, another tough decision for West whether to pull to 4♠ or pass.

East passed and West led the ◇10 against 4♡. Declarer ruffed in dummy and finessed the ♣10 successfully. Then he ruffed another diamond, returned to the ♣A and ruffed a third diamond in dummy.

Stuck in dummy, he led a third club and ruffed East's ♣K with the ♡8. Oops, West overruffed and returned a trump to dummy's ♡K. Declarer had two spades and a diamond still to lose. Down one.

What might be a better approach?

Set up a long suit. Hope for 2-2 or 3-1 trumps and ruff dummy's clubs high. After the ♣10 wins, cash the ♣A, cross to the ♡Q and ruff a club high. If all follow to the ♡J next, 12 tricks. Else low to the ♡K and 11 tricks.

Oh yes, Jim looked in his medical books but found no reference to *Compulsive Ruffing Syndrome* ("Keep ruffing as long as you can!"). We can only wonder whether anyone will discover a cure for it.

DEAL 63. SECOND SUIT OR RUFF?

```
                    ♠ Q 8 5
                    ♡ Q 9 7 5 3 2
                    ◇ A 6 3
                    ♣ A
♠ 9 7 4                              ♠ 10 3
♡ K 4                                ♡ A J 10
◇ Q J 5 2                            ◇ 10 9 7
♣ Q 9 3 2                            ♣ K 7 6 5 4
                    ♠ A K J 6 2
                    ♡ 8 6
                    ◇ K 8 4
                    ♣ J 10 8
```

North raised South's 1♠ response to 2♠, slightly better than rebidding her svelte six-card heart suit. That made it easy for South to bid 4♠.

West led the ◇ 2.

Declarer saw eight likely winners. Ruff clubs or set up the heart suit? Going for ruffs, he won the ◇A and cashed the ♣A. He entered his hand with the ◇K to ruff a club. The ♠A provided an entry to ruff his last club with dummy's ♠Q. Five tricks home, but now he was stuck in dummy with only red cards to lead.

When the defenders got in, West could give East an uppercut by leading a fourth diamond, or East could promote a trump trick for West by leading a third heart. Either way, down one.

How can you tell "second suit" deals from "take ruffs in the short hand" deals?

Look at the entries. Ample hand entries argue for taking ruffs in dummy. Ample dummy entries argue for setting up dummy's long suit.

Here you have more dummy entries. Win the opening lead in hand and start hearts. With hearts and spades both splitting 3-2, you'll make.

DEAL 64. WILL YOU STILL NEED ME, WILL YOU STILL FEED ME …

```
                    ♠ Q J 10 9
                    ♡ 9 5
                    ◇ 7
                    ♣ A K 10 6 5 2
♠ 7 4                                    ♠ 6 5
♡ Q 10 8 4                               ♡ K J 6
◇ A 9 4 2                                ◇ K J 6 8 5
♣ 8 3                                    ♣ Q J 9
                    ♠ A K 8 5 2
                    ♡ A 7 2
                    ◇ Q 10 3
                    ♣ 7 4
```

A confused "splinter" auction led South to think North had a void in diamonds when North thought he was showing a singleton, resulting in an iffy 6♠ slam.

However, six-baggers make great second suits, and 6-4 hands with ace-king-sixth make superb dummies when declarer knows to treat them as the "master hand" and ruff out the six-card side suit.

That applies here. West leads the ♡4. Count your tricks. Dummy's four trump tricks. Five club tricks if the suit splits 3-2 (it's a favorite to do so). One heart trick. Two ruffs in hand (one in clubs, one in a red suit). That makes 12.

So: ♡A, ♣A, ♠A, ♣K, club ruffed with the ♠K, ♠Q. When both defenders follow twice in each black suit, fun time begins. Discard all your diamonds on dummy's three long clubs.

Ruff a diamond and surrender a heart trick. Dummy's ♠J and ♠10 win the last two tricks.

Now you can tell your partner, "I thought you had the diamond void, but now I see that I did," and offer to discuss "splinters" with him later.

DEAL 65. ? WINNERS ? LOSERS

```
                       ♠ K J 6 4
                       ♡ Q J 10 4 2
                       ◊ 2
                       ♣ 6 4 2
     ♠ 10 3                              ♠ 5 2
     ♡ K 7                               ♡ A 9 8 5
     ◊ K Q J 10 3                        ◊ 9 8 5 4
     ♣ K J 10 8                          ♣ 9 7 3
                       ♠ A Q 9 8 7
                       ♡ 6 3
                       ◊ A 7 6
                       ♣ A Q 5
```

West overcalled 2◊ on favorable vulnerability, and South, who might have settled for a 3♠ limit raise in an uncontested auction, gambled 4♠ to make it harder for the opponents to know whether 5◊ would be a profitable save or a phantom.

South won the diamond opening lead with the ◊A and promptly ruffed a diamond. He returned to his hand with the ♠Q and ruffed his last diamond with dummy's ♠J. Dummy's ♠K drew the outstanding trumps.

In dummy for the last time, declarer finessed the ♣Q. When it lost to West's ♣K, declarer was helpless. He had to lose two hearts and another club. Down one.

By now, we trust, you are no longer a ruffaholic, so how would declare?

Recognizing this as a second-suit deal, attack hearts promptly at Trick 2 to avoid having to finesse clubs later. Ruffing diamonds can wait.

West will hop up with his ♡K to tap dummy, the "danger hand" in a different sense of the phrase (the hand with the establishable side suit).

After ruffing in dummy, lead the ♡Q. Upon winning the ♡A, East can shift to clubs, but disdaining the finesse, you can win the ♣A, draw trump with dummy's ♠K and ♠J, run hearts and take the rest, Instead of an undertrick, an overtrick.

DEAL 66. NEED IT, TAKE IT

```
              ♠ A 10 8 7 6 5
              ♡ A 6
              ◊ K 4 3
              ♣ A Q
♠ K Q 9                        ♠ J 4 2
♡ Q J 10 9 8 3                 ♡ K 7 2
◊ 6                            ◊ Q 7 5
♣ K 3 2                        ♣ J 10 9 7
              ♠ 3
              ♡ 5 4
              ◊ A J 10 9 8 2
              ♣ 8 6 5 4
```

After South's Weak 2◊ Bid and West's 2♡ overcall, North responded 2♠. When East's 3♡ raise came round to him, North gambled 6◊. With neither side vul, West did not risk a 6♡ save, especially when 6◊ might not make.

Declarer won West's ♡Q opening lead with dummy's ♡A. Trying to set up the spades, he cashed the ♠A and ruffed a spade with the ◊J. He crossed to dummy's ♣A and another spade with the ◊10. Hallelujah, the spades split 3-3.

When declarer cashed the ◊A and led low to dummy's ◊K, East ruffed with the ◊Q, the master trump. South discarded his remaining heart, but East led a club to West's ♣K for the setting trick.

Right diagnosis ("Second-Suit Deal") but the wrong operation and the patient died. Could you have saved the contract?

Yes, if you realize that the cancer has spread from the heart suit to the club suit. Too few potential spade winners to excise both tumors.

After taking the ♡A, the ♠A and a spade ruff, cash the ◊A and ◊K, but when you see that you must lose to the ◊Q, you must ruff another spade and take the club finesse while you can.

When it wins, lead dummy's spades to discard your low heart and then low clubs. East can ruff in whenever he likes, but you have the rest.

DEAL 67. PUNISHMENT

                          ♠ Q 6 3
                          ♡ 10 8 7
                          ◊ 4 3
                          ♣ A Q J 8 5
        ♠ A 9 8   ♠ 10 4
        ♡ A 5 4   ♡ K Q J 9 6 3
        ◊ Q J 10 8 7   ◊ 9 6
        ♣ 6 2   ♣ 9 4 3
                          ♠ K J 7 5 2
                          ♡ 2
                          ◊ A K 5 2
                          ♣ K 10 7

Though it would also have been reasonable to make a takeout double, South overcalled 2♠ after East opened a Weak 2♡ Bid. After a little pushing and shoving, he reached 4♠.

West led the ◊Q, top of his God-Given Sequence. "Wouldn't lead your partner's suit, eh?" said South. "Don't you trust her Weak Twos?"

West kept silent, and South silently counted 13 tricks: four spades, five clubs, two top diamonds, and two diamond ruffs in dummy.

So, ◊A, ◊K and a diamond ruff. Oops, East overruffed with the ♠4 and tried to cash the ♡K.

"I thought this might come in handy later," said West, overtaking with the ♡A to lead the ◊J.

"Never send a girl to do a woman's job," said South, taking care to ruff with dummy's ♠Q. He avoided the overruff but now West's ♠A98 turned into two tricks. South's hoped-for 13 tricks became nine. Down one.

For how many tricks would you have played if you were declaring?

By now, we hope, you'd recognize this as a "second-suit deal" and play for 10. Lead low to dummy's ♠Q at Trick 2 and back to the ♠K to drive out the ♠A. Finish trump when you regain the lead and you'll take 11 tricks.

DEAL 68. BE CAREFUL

```
                  ♠ A K J 3
                  ♡ 7 5
                  ◊ Q J 5 2
                  ♣ J 7 4
    ♠ 6 5                        ♠ 10 9 8
    ♡ K Q J 10 4                 ♡ 9 6
    ◊ K 3                        ◊ 10 9 8 6
    ♣ K 9 3 2                    ♣ Q 10 6 5
                  ♠ Q 7 4 2
                  ♡ A 8 3 2
                  ◊ A 7 4
                  ♣ A 8
```

Danny opens more four-card majors than anybody in 21st-century America, but even he would open 1◊ with South's hand. After West overcalled 1♡, North made a Negative Double to show four spades. South showed a maximum four-card raise of 1♠ to 2♠ by bidding 2♠, and North reraised to 4♠.

West led the ♡K to South's ♡A. Thinking to ruff two hearts in dummy, declarer led another heart. Oops, wrong plan.

Needing to ruff with honors both times, South promoted East's ♠1098 to a trick … the setting trick.

Do you see a better plan?

We hope you see this as a second-suit deal. Dummy's diamonds are the second suit. Draw trumps promptly and lead towards dummy's ◊QJ52. A 3-3 split or the ◊K with West will see you home.

Ten easy tricks: one heart, one club, three diamonds, three spades, and two more spades scored separately with club and heart ruffs.

DEAL 69. DON'T YIELD TO TEMPTATION

```
                    ♠ A K 8 6 5 3
                    ♡ 2
                    ◊ A 5 4
                    ♣ K 7 2
   ♠ 10 9                              ♠ Q 7 4 2
   ♡ K Q 9 7 6                         ♡ 10 8 5 4
   ◊ J 9                               ◊ Q 10 3
   ♣ Q 10 9 5                          ♣ 6 3
                    ♠ J
                    ♡ A J 3
                    ◊ K 8 7 6 2
                    ♣ A J 8 4
```

Two-Over-One Game-Forcing might make it easier to reach the good 6◊ slam, as this is the kind of deal that shows that framework to best advantage (slow bidding after a two-over-one response), but standard bidding worked at least as well after a 1♠-2◊; 2♠-3♣; 4◊ (good bid!) start.

West led the ♡K against 6◊. Declarer won the ♡A and (you guessed it!) lured by dummy's singleton, ruffed a heart immediately.

Then he cashed the ◊A and ◊K. Good luck: trumps split 3-2. Now two top spades to pitch his last heart, ruff a spade, and … West showed out, bad luck: spades split 4-2. A club finesse combined with a 3-3 club split offered a last resort, but 4-2 clubs with the ♣Q offside meant down two.

"Hmmm," mused South. "A four or six deal!"

Mr. Mephistopheles, East, grinned and blurted out, "No, a six or six deal!" What the devil did he mean by that?

Six to the ace-king in dummy makes a heavenly side suit. After winning the ♡A, lead to the ♠K and ruff a spade. Then the ◊K and low to the ◊A and ruff another spade.

Now cross to the ♣K, cash the ♠A and keep leading spades till the defender with the master trump ruffs in. You'll have discarded two clubs and a heart on spades, so a trump trick is all you'll lose.

Somehow, 6◊ is almost always a "lucky" contract.

DEAL 70. RUFFS? ANYTHING BETTER?

```
                        ♠ A 6 4
                        ♡ Q 5 3 2
                        ◊ 3
                        ♣ K 9 6 5 2
        ♠ K Q 9 8                          ♠ J 10 5
        ♡ 8 4                              ♡ 10 9
        ◊ J 10 6 5                         ◊ K Q 9 7 2
        ♣ Q 10 3                           ♣ J 8 4
                        ♠ 7 3 2
                        ♡ A K J 7 6
                        ◊ A 8 4
                        ♣ A 7
```

Wisely resisting the fashionable and supposedly sexy 1NT, South opened a girl-next-door 1♡ and bid 4♡ over North's routine limit raise.

West led the ♠K to dummy's ♠A. The rush-to-ruff declarer played the ◊A and ruffed a diamond, ♡A and ruffed his last diamond, catching his breath only to cry, "Whew, Mission One accomplished!"

When both defenders followed to dummy's ♡Q next, he cried, "Whew, Mission Two accomplished!"

Having taken the ruffs he needed in the short hand, South set about Mission Three: ruffing out dummy's clubs. ♣A, ♣K and a club ruff brought down all the missing clubs.

South displayed his hand, saying, "Dummy's clubs are good. I'll discard my remaining spades on them and the rest are trumps."

Oops, no way to reach those two good clubs. Only 11 tricks, not 13. Could you have done better?

Sure. ♠A, ♡Q, ♡A. Still time to ruff diamonds in dummy if necessary. When hearts split 2-2, ♣A, ♣K, club ruff. When clubs split 3-3, 13 tricks; if not, 4♡ still makes. Unimportant at rubber bridge, but vital at matchpoints.

Can't hurt to stay in practice, and the extra 60 points may mean a dollar at rubber bridge, Penny a point with everyone keepin' score.

DEAL 71. RUFF IN DUMMY OR SECOND SUIT?

                        ♠ Q 7 4
                        ♡ J 9 7 6 3 2
                        ◇ A 8 3
                        ♣ A

♠ 9 8 5   ♠ 10 6
♡ K 4   ♡ A Q 10
◇ Q J 10 7   ◇ 9 5 2
♣ Q 9 7 6   ♣ K 10 5 4 2

                        ♠ A K J 3 2
                        ♡ 8 5
                        ◇ K 6 4
                        ♣ J 8 3

South opened 1♠ and reached 4♠ on an uncontested auction. West led the ◇Q.

South counted eight top tricks and needed two more to make 4♠. He thought he could get them by ruffing two clubs in dummy. So, ◇A, ♣A, ruff a club. Back to the ♠A, ruff the last club … with dummy's ♠Q.

Stranded in dummy, declarer was unable to draw the remaining trumps immediately. When he came off dummy with a heart, East took the ♡A and led the ◇9 to West's ◇10.

West cashed the ♡K and led the ◇J. East was wide awake enough to uppercut by ruffing with the ♠10, and declarer had to lose a trump trick to West. Down one.

Was trying for a second suit any better? If so, why?

Remember the guiding principle: *With more hand entries, take ruffs in dummy, but with more dummy entries, try to set up dummy's suit.*

So, win Trick 1 in hand with the ◇K, duck a heart, win the diamond return with dummy's ◇A, and duck another heart. Now the best defense is for West to win the third diamond and lead a fourth for East to uppercut you.

But you'll overruff, draw trump in three rounds ending in dummy, ruff a heart with your last trump and cross to dummy to take the rest in hearts.

DEAL 72. FULL STEAM AHEAD

```
                          ♠ 9 7 4
                          ♡ A 8 2
                          ◇ A 9 6 3 2
                          ♣ 10 2
        ♠ Q 10 8                           ♠ J 6
        ♡ J 10 9 5                         ♡ Q 6 4
        ◇ J 8                              ◇ Q 10 5 4
        ♣ Q 9 8 4                          ♣ J 7 5 3
                          ♠ A K 5 3 2
                          ♡ K 7 3
                          ◇ K 7
                          ♣ A K 6
```

Because a balanced 21-HCP hand must usually be opened 2NT despite the presence of a respectable five-card major, several methods of seeking a 5-3 fit in a major exist. In the confusion that followed South's 2NT opening here, North used one method to uncover the 5-3 spade fit but South was used to another and wound up in an unlikely 6♠ slam.

West led the ♡J. Declarer crossruffed and ended with 11 tricks, losing a third-round heart trick as well as the unavoidable trump trick.

How would you tackle this ridiculous slam?

Start by assuming that you'll get the unusually good luck that you need, in particular a 3-2 trump split. The only sparkle of hope lies in diamonds, dummy's five-card suit. If you can set it up, you can discard a heart loser.

Win Trick 1 with the ♡K, retaining the ♡A as a dummy entry. Cash both top trumps, the ◇K and the ◇A, then ruff a diamond. West can overruff with the master trump and drive out dummy's ♡A, but now a second diamond ruff sets up a long diamond.

Two top clubs and a club ruff put you back in dummy, and away goes your last heart on dummy's ◇9.

DEAL 73. DOOMED FROM THE START

```
                    ♠ A K Q 6
                    ♡ 8 6 5 3 2
                    ◊ 6 5
                    ♣ 4 2
    ♠ 4 2                              ♠ 8 3
    ♡ J 10 9                          ♡ A K 7 4
    ◊ Q 9 8 4                         ◊ K 10 7 2
    ♣ K Q 10 8                        ♣ 9 6 5
                    ♠ J 10 9 7 5
                    ♡ Q
                    ◊ A J 3
                    ♣ A J 7 3
```

Playing limit jump raises, North raised South's 1♠ opening to 3♠. Having heard somewhere that opener should always bid game with a singleton, South bid 4♠. We're not so sure when the singleton is a king or queen.

South only saw three losers if he could ruff three times in dummy. So he won the ♣K opening lead with the ♣A and ducked a club. West won the ♣8 and shifted to a trump. Declarer ruffed a club, came to his ◊A and ruffed his last club.

But when he led dummy's last diamond, East rose with the ◊K and led another trump. Declarer lost a diamond and a heart; down one.

South's line was doomed from the start unless he was playing against Aunt Gertrude or Uncle Lou. Was there a line that could succeed even against Cousin Marcia?

Perhaps. Where there's five, there's hope, and dummy has five hearts. Lead the ♡Q to Trick 2. Win the trump return in dummy and ruff a heart high. Lead a club and win the trump return in dummy. Ruff another heart high. Cross to dummy with a club ruff and ruff a third heart high.

With trumps 2-2 and hearts 4-3, you have 10 tricks: two top spades, two minor-suit aces, five trumps scored ruffing, and a long lonely heart.

Even Cousin Marcia couldn't stop you.

DEAL 74. PLEASE STOP RUFFING

```
                          ♠ 5 3
                          ♡ A 5 3
                          ◊ A J 7 6 4 2
                          ♣ 6 5
        ♠ Q 10 9 2                      ♠ K 7 8 6
        ♡ 9 8                           ♡ 7 4 2
        ◊ K 9 3                         ◊ Q 10
        ♣ Q J 10 2                      ♣ A 8 7 3
                          ♠ A J 4
                          ♡ K Q J 10 6
                          ◊ 8 5
                          ♣ K 9 4
```

North liked his hand well enough to show a "three-card limit raise," starting with a forcing 1NT response and jumping to 3♡ over South's 2♣ rebid. South like his hand just well enough to carry on to 4♡.

East overtook West's ♣Q opening lead with the ♣A to shift to the ♡2. South won in hand, cashed the ♣K and ruffed his last club. But now he was in trouble.

He needed to ruff a spade in dummy, but whether he let the defenders take a first-round or second-round spade trick, a second trump lead would wreck that plan. Two spade losers and one loser in each minor meant down one.

Could you do any better than try for two ruffs in dummy?

Yes. Once East makes no effort to shorten dummy's trumps by forcing dummy to ruff, use dummy's ♡A as a late entry to the long diamonds.

Win East's trump shift with the ♡K and duck a diamond. Be sure to win a second trump lead in hand also. Now a diamond to dummy's ◊A and another diamond ruffed high will set up the suit while the ♡A remains in dummy as a late entry.

A little bit of luck, 3-2 splits in both red suits, will bring you 11 tricks and see you through.

CHAPTER 4
Ruffing Finesses

DEAL 75. UNBLOCKING

                          ♠ A K 4
                          ♡ K 4 2
                          ◇ 7 2
                          ♣ Q J 10 9 5

♠ Q J 10 9 2   ♠ 7 6 5 3
♡ 3   ♡ J 10 6
◇ K 10 8 4   ◇ J 3
♣ K 6 4   ♣ 8 7 3 2

                          ♠ 8
                          ♡ A Q 9 8 7 5
                          ◇ A Q 9 6 5
                          ♣ A

After a slow 1♡-2♣; 2◇ start, North's 3♡ was game-forcing and promised decent three-card support (♡J102 or stronger). South had visions of slam and bid 4♠, which they played as Kickback, the optimal keycard-ask for hearts.

North's 5♣ reply showed both missing keys and denied the ♡Q, and his 5NT reply to the 5♠ Specific King Ask showed the ♠K. South asked for the ◇K by bidding 6◇, and passed North's 6♡ denial.

West led the ♠Q to dummy's ♠K, removing dummy's only outside entry. Declarer banked on diamonds. He finessed the ◇Q. His hopes dimmed when West won the ◇K and returned a trump. They disappeared entirely when East overruffed the third diamond and returned another trump. Down two.

"Played like a Neanderthal," growled North. Was she right?

No. Somebody said "Diamonds are a girl's best friend," but *clubs* are a Neanderthal's best friend. North's beefy clubs are a second suit strong enough to lug the good slam home to the cave.

A Neanderthal makes 6♡. At Trick 2, pitch the blocking ♣A on dummy's ♠A. Then lead ♣Q and discard a diamond when East plays low.

West will win the ♣K, but that will be the only trick for the defense. Ruff West's spade continuation, draw trump ending in dummy and ditch those worthless diamond baubles on dummy's clubs. Ooga chukka, ooga chukka!

DEAL 76. FINESSE? WHAT FINESSE?

```
              ♠ Q 9 7 3
              ♡ Q J 8 7 4
              ◊ void
              ♣ J 7 4 3
♠ 6 4                          ♠ 10 8 5
♡ A 5 2                        ♡ K 10 6 3
◊ Q 8 6 3                      ◊ A 4 2
♣ Q 10 9 2                     ♣ K 6 5
              ♠ A K J 2
              ♡ 9
              ◊ K J 10 9 7 5
              ♣ A 8
```

After North raised South's 1♠ rebid to 2♠, South bid a reasonable 4♠.

West's ♣10 opening lead rode to South's ♣A. Thinking to crossruff, South led the ♡9 to dummy's ♡J. East won the ♡K and shifted to the ♠5.

South won the ♠A and crossruffed. He scored only three ruffs in each hand and his two black aces?

Overbid or underplayed?

Underplayed. Holding a good six-card suit with only two holes in it, take it to a tailor. Even a tailor's grandson will know what to do with it.

Lead the ◊J to Trick 2. If West holds the ◊A without the ◊Q, he may well rise for fear you have both ◊K and ◊Q. As it happens, he'll likely cover with the ◊Q.

No matter: ruff, return to your hand with a high spade, and lead the ◊K for a second ruffing diamond finesse. When West follows low, discard a heart from dummy. East will win the ◊A, but no matter.

The defenders can take that trick, a heart and a club, but you can ruff the next heart or club, finish trumps, and run diamonds to make 4♠.

DEAL 77. NOT ONCE BUT TWICE

```
                    ♠ J 4 3
                    ♡ K 10 9 8 7
                    ◇ K 9 2
                    ♣ 4 2
        ♠ K 8 2                      ♠ Q 10 7 6
        ♡ A 5 2                      ♡ J 6 4 3
        ◇ 8 7 5                      ◇ 6
        ♣ K 9 8 7                    ♣ Q 10 6 3
                    ♠ A 9 5
                    ♡ Q
                    ◇ A Q J 10 4 3
                    ♣ A J 5
```

North responded 1♡ but wasn't quite sure what to do over South's jump 3◇ rebid. He settled on 4◇ hoping South could put him in 4♡ with honor-third support and retreated to 5◇ when South cue-bid 4♠ instead.

West rejected an attacking lead in favor of a passive trump. Declarer won the ◇A and led the ♡Q. West paused briefly before playing the ♡2, and South's ♡Q won.

"That's an ugly duckling," quipped East. Eventually South lost two spades and a club. Down one.

"Pass four diamonds if you're going to mess up the play," said North.

Was North right? Could *you* make 5◇?

Half right, half wrong. 4◇ was forcing. After an invitational jump in a previously shown suit, any further bid accepts game. But yes, you can make 5◇ after a trump lead.

You must flush out the ♡A *and* the ♡J. Overtake the ♡Q with dummy's ♡K. If it wins, you're in dummy for the first of *two* ruffing finesses. If it loses, you only need one.

Either way, you have enough trump entries, and in time, discards enough for your black-suit losers. And oh yes, the "ugly duckling" was a actually swan.

DEAL 78. SUBTERFUGE

```
                    ♠ 9 4 2
                    ♡ Q 10 9 6 3
                    ◊ Q 6
                    ♣ J 10 4
    ♠ K 7 6                         ♠ Q J 10 3
    ♡ 8 5                           ♡ 4
    ◊ J 10 9 7                      ◊ K 5 4
    ♣ A 8 6 3                       ♣ K 9 7 5 2
                    ♠ A 8 5
                    ♡ A K J 7 2
                    ◊ A 8 3 2
                    ♣ Q
```

South reached 4♡ via a simple 1♡–2♡–4♡ auction. West led the ◊J.

Declarer tried dummy's ◊Q, but East's ◊K dislodged his ◊A. Then South led the ♣Q, which rode to East's ♣K. East shifted to the ♠Q.

Declarer was soon down one.

Would you have seen your best hope of making?

Instead of leading the ♣Q, cross to dummy's ♡9 and lead the ♣4. If East plays low, West will win the ♣A.

Now you can take a ruffing finesse through East's ♣K to set up a club trick in dummy, on which you can discard a spade loser.

Yes, East could thwart this plan by rising with the ♣K, but how many Easts, even among those who read Jim and Danny's book on "Second Hand High," would find this spectacular defense?

CHAPTER 5
Ruffs and Overruffs

DEAL 79. AVOIDING THE OVERRUFF

```
                         ♠ K 8
                         ♡ A Q 2
                         ◊ A 6 4
                         ♣ A 6 5 4 3
        ♠ Q 10 6 4 2                      ♠ J 9 7 5 3
        ♡ J 10 9                          ♡ 8
        ◊ 9 8 7                           ◊ K Q 10
        ♣ J 9                             ♣ Q 10 8 7
                         ♠ A
                         ♡ K 7 6 5 4 3
                         ◊ J 5 3 2
                         ♣ K 2
```

Hands like North's are notorious for being hard to bid "scientifically." They contain too many fine features to show easily. When South opened 1♡ and rebid 2♡ over his 2♣, North gambled sensibly by jumping to 6♡. West led the ♠4.

Declarer won the ♠A, and realizing that he might need a trump entry to dummy to ruff out clubs, cashed only the ♡A and ♡K before starting trump in three rounds before working on clubs.

Alas, West still had the ♡J. When South took the ♣K, led to dummy's ♣A and ruffed a club, West overruffed and shifted to diamonds. Declarer won dummy's ◊A and ruffed another club.

But with only two discards coming, on dummy's ♠K and fifth club, he still had a diamond to lose in the end. Down one.

Could you have set up the clubs while avoiding the overruff?

Yes. By taking your first club ruff on the second round of the suit while both defenders must follow. At Tricks 2 and 3, cash the ♡K and the ♣K, cross to the ♡A and discard the remaining club on the ♠K.

Then ruff a club, draw the last trump with dummy's ♡Q, discard a diamond on dummy's ♣A, and ruff another club. Then you can cross to dummy's ◊A to discard a second diamond on the long club. Making 6♡. no sweat.

DEAL 80. SECOND SUIT TO COMPRESS YOUR LOSERS

```
                      ♠ K 3
                      ♡ A 2
                      ◊ A 8 6 4 2
                      ♣ J 8 7 3
      ♠ 10 6                          ♠ J 9 4 2
      ♡ J 10 6 5                      ♡ K Q 9 7 4
      ◊ J 10 9 7 3                    ◊ K Q
      ♣ A 2                           ♣ K 5
                      ♠ A Q 8 7 5
                      ♡ 8 3
                      ◊ 5
                      ♣ Q 10 9 6 4
```

East opened 1♡ and South bid 2♡, an Ambiguous Michaels Cue Bid showing spades and an unknown minor. West stretched to raise to 3♡ and North, having support for both minors, bid 4NT to ask South to bid his.

West led the ♡J against South's 5♣. Needing to discard a heart loser, declarer won dummy's ♡A and ♠K, then came to his ♠A and tried to cash the ♠Q hoping to discard dummy's ♡2.

Alas, before he could discard dummy's ♡2, West "discarded" the ♣2. After overruffing in dummy, South led dummy's ♣J. Forgetting his Mother Goose, East failed to cover an honor with an honor. West won the ♣A, and East took the setting tricks with the ♡Q and the ♣K.

Was there any way to avoid three losers?

Yes, by compressing two trump losers into one. After the ruff and overruff at Trick 4, cash dummy's ◊A and ruff a diamond. West dare not ruff with the ♣A, else you can discard dummy's ♡2, so he'll discard.

Ruff another diamond and lead your fifth spade to discard dummy's ♡2. If West ruffs, it's with his ♣A.

If East ruffs, you'll ruff his heart exit in dummy and lead a trump. The ♣K and ♣A will fall together, and their crash will echo in the next room.

One way or another, you'll make 5♣, losing only two trump tricks.

DEAL 81. PLEASE STOP TRUMPING MY WINNERS

                        ♠ K 7 6 2
                        ♡ 10 2
                        ◇ A J 10 6 3
                        ♣ A K
      ♠ 4   ♠ 9 8 5 3
      ♡ Q J 8 7   ♡ 4
      ◇ 9 7 2   ◇ K Q 8 5
      ♣ Q J 10 7 3   ♣ 9 6 5 2
                        ♠ A Q J 10
                        ♡ A K 9 6 5 3
                        ◇ 4
                        ♣ 8 4

South opened 1♡ and North bid 2◇. South "reversed" into 2♠, which they played as showing substantial extras even when 2◇ was game-forcing. That made it easy for North to bid 6♠ without further ado.

West led the ♣Q to dummy's ♣K. Declarer cashed the ♠Q and ♠J. Upon seeing West show out, he played hearts from the top. Alas, East ruffed the second heart and exited with his last trump.

South could ruff only one heart in dummy, and his remaining hearts, not yet established, went to waste. Three wasted hearts meant down three.

A nightmare deal, 4-1 splits in both key suits. Any remedy?

Yes. Fortunately, the contract is 6♠, not 7♠. After winning the ♣K, lead to the ♡A and cash only the ♠Q, then surrender a heart.

Win the return, lead to the ♠J and ruff a heart with dummy's ♠K. Draw the remaining trumps and now the hearts will run from the top.

DEAL 82. KEEPING CONTROL IN A STORM

```
                        ♠ 3
                        ♡ K Q 10 7
                        ◇ A K 9 4 3 2
                        ♣ 7 3
        ♠ K 9 8                             ♠ A J 10 7 5
        ♡ 5                                 ♡ 8 6 3 2
        ◇ Q J 8 6                           ◇ 10
        ♣ K Q 10 8 4                        ♣ J 9 5
                        ♠ Q 6 4 2
                        ♡ A J 9 4
                        ◇ 7 5
                        ♣ A 6 2
```

Adverse vulnerability deterred East and West from entering the auction after North opened 1◇ and South responded 1♡. North had more than enough to invite game with 3♡, and South had more than enough to bid 4♡.

West led the ♣ K. Declarer saw only two likely losers. He took his two aces and led a second heart to dummy's ♡Q. He stopped to think when West showed out.

Needing to establish dummy's diamonds, he led them from the top ◇AK. East ruffed the second diamond and led his last trump to kill dummy.

Could you have navigated your way through this storm of 4-1 splits?

In his excellent syndicated *Daily Bridge Column*, Frank Stewart offered "a valuable principle of declarer play: When the play may be a struggle - maybe keeping control of your trump suit is an issue - establish your side suit and start early."

Here you'll do well to start diamonds at Trick 2. East will ruff the second of dummy's top diamonds and the defenders may take two top tricks in the black suits, but whether they do so or shift to trumps promptly, you'll ruff out and run diamonds, using dummy's trump honors for entries.

Not the 11 tricks for which you may have hoped, but the 10 tricks that you need. Thanks, Frank.

DEAL 83. A SIMILAR PROBLEM

```
                    ♠ A Q 9 7
                    ♡ A K Q 8 5 2
                    ◇ 9
                    ♣ K 2
   ♠ 6 5 3 2                        ♠ 4
   ♡ 4                              ♡ J 10 9 3
   ◇ 6 3                            ◇ K Q J 10
   ♣ Q J 9 7 5 4                    ♣ 10 8 6 3
                    ♠ K J 10 8
                    ♡ 7 6
                    ◇ A 8 7 5 4 2
                    ♣ A
```

South opened 1◇, and North did well to refrain from bidding 2♡, as strong jump shifts should not include nice four-card side suits that might be the best trump suits for slam. However, when South rebid 1♠ over his 1♡, North had just the tool he needed to place the contract:

Roman Keycard Blackwood. RKB requires a known trump suit, and as North did *not* bid 2♡ initially that suit could only be spades.

South's 5♣ reply to the RKB 4NT confirmed all three missing keys, and not having mastered Danny's jack-ask adjunct to RKB (even Danny has trouble remembering it!), North risked 7♠ without knowledge of the ♠J.

West led the ♣Q. South won and took both trump monarchs, getting the first bad news. The 4-1 spade split meant he could handle a 4-1 heart split only if West had the four, so he tried to cash two top hearts next. West ruffed. Down one.

"Déjà vu all over again," said the kibitzer they called Yogi (not his real name). What did he mean by that?

Just two rubbers earlier, Yogi had seen a declarer fail in 6♡ by neglecting to discard from a doubleton in a suit he hoped to ruff out.

Here South could prevail in 7♠ by discarding a heart on dummy's ♣K and cashing only one top heart before ruffing a heart.

"Why does déjà vu come only in pairs?" said Yogi. "Is it like kudos?"

DEAL 84. AVOIDING THE OVERRUFF

                          ♠ A Q 3
                          ♡ K 2
                          ◊ K 6 5 4 3
                          ♣ A 6 4
        ♠ J 10 9   ♠ 8
        ♡ Q 10 8 6 3   ♡ J 9 7 5 4
        ◊ J 7   ◊ Q 10 9 8
        ♣ K 10 9   ♣ Q 8 7
                          ♠ K 7 6 5 4 2
                          ♡ A
                          ◊ A 2
                          ♣ J 5 3 2

South opened 1♠ and North bid 2◊, which they played as forcing to game. When South bid 2♠. North jumped to 4♠, taking advantage of a subtle merit of Two-Over-One Game-Forcing. As 3♠ would still be forcing, 4♠ showed extras in the form of surprisingly strong three-card support. South's 5◊ cue bid next was all that North needed to bid 6♠.

Fearing to lead from a king, especially against a slam, West led a "safe" ♠J. Declarer realized he needed dummy's ♠Q as a late entry to cash a diamond or two after ruffing out dummy's five-card suit.

He cashed only the ♠A and ♠K, then continued with the ◊A and ◊K and ruffed a diamond. Alas, West overruffed with the ♠10 and exited in hearts. Eventually, his ♣K took the setting trick.

Could you have avoided the disaster that befell poor South?

Well, yes. Win the ♠K at Trick 1 and unblock both red aces. Cross to dummy's ♠Q, discard the ◊2 on dummy's ♡K, and ruff a diamond on the second round with less danger of an overruff.

Draw West's last trump with dummy's ♠Q, discard a club on the ◊K, ruff another diamond, and back to dummy's ♣A to discard another club on dummy's fifth diamond.

"Gee," said Yogi, who was still kibitzing a rubber later. "Maybe déjà vus come in trios too."

DEAL 85. OH LORD, STUCK IN THE DUMMY AGAIN

```
                        ♠ A J 6 2
                        ♡ A 4 2
                        ◇ 6
                        ♣ A K J 10 5
        ♠ 7 4                             ♠ K Q 10 9 3
        ♡ 10 8 6                          ♡ 9
        ◇ 10 9 8 5 4 2                    ◇ K Q 7
        ♣ 8 4                             ♣ Q 9 7 2
                        ♠ 8 5
                        ♡ K Q J 7 5 3
                        ◇ A J 3
                        ♣ 6 3
```

When South opened 1♡ as dealer, North set his sights on slam and started with 2♣, which they played as game-forcing. East's 2♠ overcall put a damper on North's grand slam hopes. but when North was able to torture a diamond cue bid from South, he bid 6♡ confidently.

West led the ♠7 to dummy's ♠A, and thought to ruff his two low diamonds in dummy. ◇A, diamond ruff, low heart to the ♡K (saying a silent prayer of thanks to the Great Shuffler in the Sky when both defenders followed), and another diamond ruff ... with dummy's ♡A.

Oops, how to get back to his hand to draw the rest of the trumps? He cashed both of dummy's top clubs and continued with the ♣J. East covered with the ♣Q and South ruffed. West overruffed and returned a spade to East. Down one.

"If you'd read Jim and Danny's 'Loser-on-Loser' book you'd have made it," said North. Was he right, or was he Danny wearing a beard in disguise and trying to drum up sales for the book?

Neither. Too late for loser-on-loser now! West can pitch the ♠3 and overruff the ♠K next. But having few hand entries, South does better to work on dummy's clubs.

At Trick 2, lead low to the ♡K. Then ♣K, ♣A, ♣J. If West covers, ruff high, ♡J, ♡A and run clubs for 12 tricks. Only if West ducks does "Loser on loser" apply. Dump the ♠8 and lose only the current trick to the ♣Q or a ruff.

DEAL 86. PROTECTING YOUR SECOND SUIT

                    ♠ A K 10 8 6 3
                    ♡ A K 8 7 5 3
                    ◊ 7
                    ♣ void
    ♠ 2   ♠ Q J 7 5
    ♡ J 10 6   ♡ 4
    ◊ 10 9   ◊ K Q J 6 3
    ♣ A K Q 9 7 4 3   ♣ J 10 5
                    ♠ 9 4
                    ♡ Q 9 2
                    ◊ A 8 5 4 2
                    ♣ 8 6 2

Three-club and three-diamond openings bring trouble to both sides. To opener's partner, as he can seldom judge whether to convert to 3NT. To the opponents, who have no way to show all three possible two-suiters.

Both pairs had agreements to handle this situation. East and West played 3♣ and 3◊ opening as showing running suits when vul or in fourth seat, else suits missing one high honor. Versus either 3♣ or 3◊, North and South used 4◊ to show both majors and 4♣ to show the unbid minor and an unspecified major for which partner could then ask.

West opened 3♣ on adverse vulnerability, South replied 4♡ to North's 4◊ and bid 6♡ when North invited slam with 5♡.

South ruffed the club lead in dummy, cashed the ♡K and ♡Q, led to the ♠K and tried the ♠A---oops, West ruffed. East still had the ♠QJ. Able to ruff only one of them, South went down.

How would you play to give yourself a better chance?

The bidding suggests bad breaks. At Trick 2, cash the ♡A and ♠A, then come to your ◊A. Now lead your last spade.

If West ruffs air, you can draw his last trump and ruff the spades good. If he discards, win the ♠K, ruff a spade high, ruff a diamond in dummy and ruff another spade. West can overruff but you have the rest.

93

CHAPTER 6
Timing

DEAL 87. THE DEVIL TAKES ANOTHER SOUL

```
                    ♠ K 4
                    ♡ A 7 4
                    ◊ 5 3
                    ♣ A K 9 5 3 2        The Devil
    ♠ 10 9 5 2                           ♠ 8 6
    ♡ Q 9 5                              ♡ J 10 6 3
    ◊ K 10 7 2                           ◊ J 9 8 6
    ♣ J 7                                ♣ Q 10 6
                    ♠ A Q J 7 3
                    ♡ K 8 2
                    ◊ A Q 4
                    ♣ 8 4
```

Finding no eight-card fit, but having more than ordinary game values, South tried for slam with 4NT. As often happens, North interpreted 4NT as a keycard ask in spades and bid 5♣, whereupon South bid 6♠.

West led the ♡5. Counting 12 tricks via a winning diamond finesse followed by a diamond ruff in dummy, South rose with dummy's ♡A to finesse the ◊Q. It lost and he went down one.

"Would you like a mulligan?" offered the Devil. "Remember my terms: if you fail on the second try, your soul is mine."

South tried again. He won the opening lead in dummy and played the ♣AK and ruffed a club. West overruffed. So much for Plan B, and so much for declarer, whose neighbors saw him carted away in the Devil's own bright red paddy wagon promptly at 6:66 PM that evening.

Your turn! How would you declare? Are you going to the Devil also, or will you leave poor South to make the agonizing journey alone?

Win the opening lead in hand with the ♡K and duck a club at Trick 2. Then you'll hear the Devil mutter "Curses!" under his breath as he wins the first club and shifts to diamonds. You'll win the ◊A, draw trump, and run clubs to take the rest.

DEAL 88. TIMING

```
                    ♠ J 10 6
                    ♡ A J 9 8 7 5
                    ◇ A 10 4
                    ♣ 8                    The Devil
        ♠ 3                                ♠ A 2
        ♡ 6 4                              ♡ K Q 10 2
        ◇ K J 9 7 6 5 3                    ◇ 2
        ♣ J 10 9                           ♣ K 7 6 5 3 2
                    ♠ K Q 9 8 7 5 4
                    ♡ 3
                    ◇ Q 8
                    ♣ A Q 4
```

West's favorable-vulnerability 3◇ opening goaded North into a "bold" 3♡ overcall. South forced with 3♠, which North raised dutifully to 4♠. Two cue bids later, South bid 6♠. West ignored East's "Lightner" double and led a normal ♣J.

Allowed to win the ♣Q, South led the ♠4 to dummy's ♠10 at Trick 2. East won the ♠A and led the ◇2. West's ◇J forced dummy's ◇A and dummy's ♠J drew the last missing trump.

Only then did South turn his attention to dummy's six hearts. He cashed the ♡A and tried to ruff out the suit. Had hearts split 2-2, he could have done so and ruffed his low club with dummy's ♠6 to run it.

But alas, hearts split a much more likely 4-2. Two dummy entries short, South had no way to set up hearts and no place to park his annoying ◇8. Down one.

Could you have timed the play better?

Setting up the hearts is Job One! At Trick 2, lead to the ♡A and ruff a heart with the ♠7. Then lead the ♠8 to dummy's ♠10. East can win the ♠A and shift to the ◇2 to dislodge dummy's ◇A.

But you'll ruff a second heart, lead to dummy's ♠J to draw the last trump, and ruff a third heart to set up the suit. You can ruff the ♣4 with dummy's last trump to cash dummy's last two hearts.

DEAL 89. TIMING THE RACE

```
                    ♠ J 9 8 4
                    ♡ 10
                    ◊ K 8 4
                    ♣ K Q 10 9 6
   ♠ 6 3                              ♠ A 7
   ♡ K 9 4 2                          ♡ A J 8 6 5
   ◊ Q 6 3                            ◊ J 10 9 7
   ♣ 8 7 5 3                          ♣ A 4
                    ♠ K Q 10 5 2
                    ♡ Q 7 3
                    ◊ A 5 2
                    ♣ J 2
```

With both sides vulnerable, East opened 1♡ and South overcalled 1♠. North gambled 4♠ directly over West's 2♡ raise.

West led the ♡2 against 4♠. East won the ♡A and shifted to the ◊J. South won the ◊A and led the ♠K to East's ♠A. East's ◊9 continuation drove out dummy's ◊K.

A second spade drew the missing trumps, but when East got in again with the ♣A, he led the ◊10 to West's ◊Q, sinking the contract.

"You must run a little faster, partner," said North. "You can't afford to lose this race."

What did he mean by that? Could you win this race?

The race was for a third-round diamond trick. To win it, you must set up dummy's clubs for a diamond discard. Lead the ♣J to Trick 3 to drive out East's ♣A. He'll continue diamonds to drive out dummy's ◊K, and ruff dummy's third club when you try to cash it for a diamond discard.

But you'll overruff and ruff a heart in dummy. East can ruff again, but this time he must do so with his ♠A, and you'll dump your last diamond anyway.

DEAL 90. PLAN AHEAD

```
                    ♠ void
                    ♡ A K 10 6 5 3
                    ◊ 10 9
                    ♣ K 8 6 4 3
♠ 8 5 4 2                              ♠ A Q J 10 7 6
♡ 8 7 4                                ♡ Q J 9 2
◊ A Q 5 3                              ◊ 8 2
♣ 7 2                                  ♣ 9
                    ♠ K 9 3
                    ♡ void
                    ◊ K J 7 6 4
                    ♣ A Q J 10 5
```

North responded 1♡ to South's 1◊ opening. When South rebid 2♣ over East's 1♠ overcall next, North cue-bid 2♠. East doubled to express his belief that he could 2♠. South rebid 3♣ to show a fifth club. That impressed North sufficiently to bid 6♣ forthwith. West thought he had two diamond tricks but kindly refrained from doubling because North was his girlfriend.

Declarer ruffed the opening lead in dummy. Heeding the advice he had been given about taking ruffs in dummy, he entered his hand with trumps twice to ruff his remaining spades in dummy.

He discarded diamonds on dummy's top hearts; unlucky, the missing heart honors didn't fall. He let dummy's ◊10 ride for a finesse; unlucky again, the ◊Q was off side. Down one.

"Why didn't you double, Sweetheart?" said East, who was definitely not West's girlfriend. "You had him beaten in your own hand."

What excuse would you give if you were West? (Hint: neither "I feared you'd revoke!" nor "Because dummy is my girlfriend!" will wash.)

Say, "Never double a cold contract!" Yes, 6♣ rolls home if declarer plays to set up dummy's long side suit. At Trick 2, ruff a heart. Draw trump with the ♣A and ♣K, throw diamonds on the ♡A and ♡K, and ruff a second heart in hand.

Ruff a spade back to dummy, two long hearts to discard more diamonds, lose a "finesse" of the ◊K to West's ◊A, and crossruff the rest to make 6♣.

DEAL 91. IN THE RIGHT ORDER

```
                    ♠ K 9 8 6
                    ♡ 8 3 2
                    ◊ A K 7 6
                    ♣ Q J
    ♠ 4 3 2                         ♠ 7 5
    ♡ 10 9 7 6                      ♡ A K J 5
    ◊ Q 9 3                         ◊ J 10 4
    ♣ A 6 3                         ♣ 8 7 5 2
                    ♠ A Q J 10
                    ♡ Q 4
                    ◊ 8 5 2
                    ♣ K 10 9 4
```

Forgetting his partnership agreement to play 1♣ as Stayman, North responded 1◊, but when South rebid 1♠ he raised to 4♠, somehow achieving a normal auction.

West led the ♡10. East took the ♡K and ♡A but declarer ruffed the ♡J next. She drew trump in three rounds, pausing only to mark "100" honors on her scorepad. Time to attack clubs? Yes! She led low to dummy's ♣Q, looking surprised when she won, as West played the ♣3 and East the ♣8.

"Oh, I see I'm playing with two real gentlemen here," she said.

But when South continued with dummy's ♣J, West won the ♣A, saying, "The same courtesy doesn't apply to knaves."

The 3-3 diamond split let declarer escape for down one.

"What happened to your ten tricks?" asked North. Do you know?

Bad timing. South must not draw the last trump. After cashing two spade honors, she had to start clubs, the second suit, leading to the ♣Q and overtaking dummy's ♣J with her ♣K to drive out the ♣A while she still has a trump entry to her hand.

Notice the importance of the defenders' ducking the first club when declarer does the wrong thing, and how count signals can help them do it.

DEAL 92. WHICH SUIT?

```
                        ♠ K 6 5 2
                        ♡ A 10
                        ◊ Q 4
                        ♣ Q 7 5 4 2
        ♠ Q 10 8                        ♠ J 9 7
        ♡ 5 3 2                         ♡ 6 4
        ◊ 9 8 5 2                       ◊ A K J 7
        ♣ 9 6 3                         ♣ K J 10 8
                        ♠ A 4 3
                        ♡ K Q J 9 8 7
                        ◊ 10 6 3
                        ♣ A
```

After East doubled North's 1♠ response for takeout, the opening side marched to game via 2♡, 3♡ and 4♡.

South opened 1♡ and North bid 1♠. When South bid 2♡, North invited with 3♡. South bid 4♡ and West led the ◊ 2.

West led the ◊9. After winning the ◊J, East shifted to a trump to prevent a diamond ruff.

Facing three possible diamond losers and a spade loser, declarer pondered the dummy. Second suit? Clubs? Not enough entries. Hoping the opponents were brain dead, he led another diamond. East won and returned another trump. Down one.

South said, "How could you bid a second time with all that junk?"
"How could you go down in four hearts?" retorted North.

A better question: how could South have made four hearts?

South was right to ponder setting up a trick in a second suit, but failed to recognize the more promising second suit. Clubs needed a miracle, but spades needed only a 3-3 split.

Not a favorite, but with 36% chances, not much of a longshot either. Duck a spade at Trick 3 and hope for the best. Sometimes you luck out.

DEAL 93. GOOD TIMING

                    ♠ A 6 3
                    ♡ K 6
                    ◊ K 9 7 6 2
                    ♣ A 10 5
    ♠ 7 4   ♠ 8 5
    ♡ Q 8 4 3   ♡ J 9 7 2
    ◊ Q 10 5   ◊ A J 8 3
    ♣ J 8 7 3   ♣ Q 9 2
                    ♠ K Q J 10 9 2
                    ♡ A 10 5
                    ◊ 4
                    ♣ K 6 4

South opened 1♠ and North bid 2◊, which they played as forcing to game. One merit of "2/1 GF" is to let North to show his spade support cheaply with 3♠; standard bidders must jump to bid 4♠ for fear of getting passed in 3♠. Alas, confusion arose when South bid 3NT. Was it "Serious 3NT" or "Non-Serious 3NT"? We think it should simply *keep the ball rolling*.

Too shy to lead from his unescorted ♡Q, West led a passive ♠4.

South rushed to ruff a heart in dummy early, and after five tricks he had only his four minor-suit cards and four spades left. At last he tackled diamonds. When he lost dummy's ◊K to East's ◊A, he had to lose a club in the end. Down one.

"Good thing you ruffed that heart so early," said North.

How could you avoid the sting of such sarcasm?

By setting up a second suit---dummy's diamonds---promptly. A heart ruff can wait, but the diamonds can't. Win the ♠K at Trick 1 and lead the ◊4. You may know a West who would duck with ace-fourth or fifth, but we don't. So if West plays low, cover his card gently.

East can win a cheap trick and continue spades. When West follows, overtake your ♠9 with dummy's ♠A. Diamond ruff, back to the ♡K, another diamond ruff, ♡A and ruff a heart, ruff a third diamond and voila!

The ◊A falls and a club to dummy's ♣A lets you throw a club on dummy's long diamond to make 6♠.

DEAL 94. ONE OR THE OTHER

                        ♠ K 7
                        ♡ A K 5
                        ◊ 8 5
                        ♣ Q 9 8 5 4 2
        ♠ 6 5 2   ♠ 8 4
        ♡ J 10   ♡ 9 8 7 4
        ◊ A K 10 6 3   ◊ J 7 4 2
        ♣ K 6 3   ♣ A J 10
                        ♠ A Q J 10 9 3
                        ♡ Q 6 3 2
                        ◊ Q 9
                        ♣ 7

Would you open 1♠ with the South hand? A Weak 2♠ Bid, perhaps? Or just pass, and hope to strut your stuff later? Mr. Mealymouth, a panelist in ACBL District 23's bidding forum, says "It depends ..." We're still looking for a three-sided coin to flip. South opened 1♠ and reached 4♠ easily.

West cashed the ◊AK and switched to the ♡J. Declarer won dummy's ♡K and drew trump. He ran all his trumps but East kept ♡987 and the ♣A.

Declarer lost a heart and a club in the end. Down one.

Yes, hearts might have split 3-3 or East might have discarded badly, the defense might have erred, but do you see any other hope?

Where there's a second suit, there's hope. Here there's clubs. Win Trick 3 in hand and lead the ♣7. East can win the ♣10 and lead a heart to dummy's ♡K. Ruff a club high, cross to dummy's ♠K, and ruff another club.

When the ♣A and ♣K fall together, draw a third trump, cross to dummy's ♡A, and claim.

Were clubs not 3-3, you could then try for 3-3 hearts. Two side suits are better than one.

DEAL 95. TIMING; WIN OR FINESSE?

```
                    ♠ 8 6 5 4 2
                    ♡ A K 10
                    ◊ 8 6 2
                    ♣ A 3
      ♠ K 10 9 3                       ♠ Q J
      ♡ 7 3                            ♡ 6 2
      ◊ 10 7 4                         ◊ K Q J 5
      ♣ J 7 5 4                        ♣ K 9 8 6 2
                    ♠ A 7
                    ♡ Q J 9 8 5 4
                    ◊ A 9 3
                    ♣ Q 10
```

South opened 1♡ and rebid 2♡ over North's 1♠ response. Unlike a 2♡ rebid over a 2♣ or 2◊ response that gives opener little else to rebid cheaply, this 2♡ rebid promises a sixth heart. Prime values and splendid three-card support justified North's jump to 4♡.

West led the ♣4. Hoping West had led from the ♣K, declarer played low from dummy. However, East won the ♣K, shifted to the ◊K and declarer was helpless to avoid one spade and two diamond losers. Down one.

Bad luck? Overbid?

No, the word is *overlooked*. South chose a 50% "finesse" for his contract but overlooked a 75% *parlay*: spades no worse than 4-2 (84%) and hearts no worse than 3-1 (90%). When you need more than one good thing to happen, the probability is the product of the individual probabilities.

Here you must keep a step ahead of the defenders. Before they can get in to lead diamonds, start spades. ♣A, ♠A, another spade. East can win and cash the ♣K, but then his ◊K shift will come too late to harm you.

You'll win the ◊A and cross to dummy twice to ruff two spades. A third trump to dummy let's you discard a diamond loser on dummy's fifth spade.

Bad luck? Yes, a little bit of bad luck too, as 3-3 spades would yield an overtrick. But playing West for the ♣K would be right only in 6♠ needing a *three-legged* parlay (including also *3-3* spades and 2-0 or 3-1 hearts).

DEAL 96. TRUMP TROUBLE? SECOND SUIT FIRST

```
                    ♠ 8 5 3 2
                    ♡ 10 3
                    ◊ K 3
                    ♣ Q 9 5 4 2
     ♠ K J 6                        ♠ A Q 9 7 4
     ♡ J 8 6 5                      ♡ 9 7
     ◊ J 9 5 2                      ◊ 10 6
     ♣ K 6                          ♣ J 10 8 7
                    ♠ 10
                    ♡ A K Q 4 2
                    ◊ A Q 8 7 4
                    ♣ A 3
```

North bypassed her "Fibonacci" spade miniskirt (Danny won't let Jim call it a "suit") sensibly to respond 1NT, and took a 3♡ preference over South's 3◊ jump shift. South's 4♡ ended the auction.

East won West's low-spade lead with the ♠A. South ruffed East's ♠4 return and West unblocked the ♠K. South cashed three top trumps. Leaving West with the master trump, South cashed the ◊K, ◊A and ◊Q. No luck there either, as West remained with the ◊J.

Declarer led a fourth diamond. West won his two red jacks and led his carefully-preserved ♠J. East had discarded down to ♠Q97. He overtook and took the rest. Down three.

"Sorry, dear," said South. "I should have cashed the ace of clubs to hold the set to down two."

Was his apology adequate?

No. Anticipating 4-2 splits, he could retain control by starting his side suit first, often an effective plan when a slow trump loser may loom. Before touching trumps: ◊K, ◊A and a diamond ruff with dummy's ♡10.

Maybe a defender with a doubleton won't be able to overruff, or he'll ruff harmlessly with a trump winner. When dummy's ♡10 holds, it's trump-drawing time. Three top hearts then diamonds from the top, and 4♡ comes rolling home.

DEAL 97. SAVING A TEMPO

```
                        ♠ K 5 4
                        ♡ 9 6
                        ◊ K J 7 3 2
                        ♣ A J 3
        ♠ Q J 3                         ♠ 9
        ♡ 8 7 3                         ♡ K Q J 10 5 2
        ◊ 10 5                          ◊ Q 9 4
        ♣ 9 8 7 6 2                     ♣ K Q 10
                        ♠ A 10 8 7 6 2
                        ♡ A 4
                        ◊ A 8 6
                        ♣ 5 4
```

After North responded 2◊ to South's 1♠ opening, East overcalled 2♡, but that did not impede the North-South march to 4♠.

Declarer won the heart lead, drew two rounds of trump, cashed the ◊A, and finessed the ◊J. East won the ◊Q, cashed the ♡10 and led the ♣K to drive out dummy's ♣A.

West ruffed dummy's ◊K with the master trump and led a club to East. South lost a diamond, a heart, a diamond ruff and a club. Down one.

Could you have saved this unlucky contract?

Yes, by saving a tempo.

After learning of the trump loser, you must avoid losing a diamond trick *early*. Take dummy's ◊K and return to your hand with the ◊A.

If both defenders follow, even if the ◊Q hasn't fallen, or if East has shown out, lead low to dummy's ◊J. A defender who still has the ◊Q will win it.

But with the ♣A standing guard in dummy, you can discard your club loser on a diamond winner in time.

DEAL 98. EARLY PREPARATION

```
              ♠ A 9 6 5 3
              ♡ K 10 4
              ◊ A 8
              ♣ 9 6 5
♠ Q 7                        ♠ K J 10 8
♡ 7 5 3                      ♡ 9
◊ K Q J 2                    ◊ 9 7 6 5 4
♣ Q 8 7 2                    ♣ K 10 4
              ♠ 4 2
              ♡ A Q J 8 6 2
              ◊ 10 3
              ♣ A J 3
```

South opened 1♡ and rebid 2♡ over North's 1♠ response. North had an easy raise to 4♡.

The contract didn't look so easy when West led the ◊ K and declarer saw the duplicated lengths in clubs and diamonds. Declarer counted nine tricks and thought to set up a tenth by ruffing out dummy's spades. He won the ◊A, cashed the ♠A and ducked a spade.

East overtook West's ♠Q with the ♠K and shifted to the ♡9. Declarer let it ride to dummy's ♡10, taking care to preserve his ♡2, and ruffed a spade high.

He reentered dummy with the ♡K and ruffed another spade high, but all his dummy entries were gone. Though he still had the ♡2 in his hand, West's ♡7 stood guard to keep dummy's ♡4 from becoming an entry.

Unable to reach dummy's long spade, declarer won only the nine tricks counted at the start. Down one.

Do you see how to do better?

Retain dummy's ♠A as an entry to reach dummy when it will do you the most good. You need it to ruff the third round of spades. That means using it on the *second* round of the suit, not the first.

Duck a spade at Trick 2, not Trick 3, and your timing will work out just fine.

CHAPTER 7
Hidden Suits And Choice Of Suits

DEAL 99. OBSCURE, BUT YOUR ONLY CHANCE

                     ♠ A K 4
                     ♡ 6 4 2
                     ◇ 9 7 6 2
                     ♣ 9 7 5
    ♠ 7 6   ♠ 8 5 3
    ♡ Q J 7 3   ♡ K 10 9 8
    ◇ K 10 3   ◇ Q J 5
    ♣ J 10 8 3   ♣ Q 4 2
                     ♠ Q J 10 9 2
                     ♡ A 5
                     ◇ A 8 4
                     ♣ A K 6

South reached 4♠ via a 1♠ – 2♠ – 4♠ auction. West led ♡ Q.

Declarer counted his tricks. Five spade tricks in hand, one heart, one diamond, and two clubs. He counted them again; still only nine. Nothing to ruff in dummy for a tenth. He won the opening lead in dummy, finished trumps, looked at the ceiling for inspiration, and finished down one.

Can you find inspiration or anything else to scrape up a tenth trick?

S.J. Simon famously derided "four to the umpty"; Danny calls it a miniskirt, but even an "itsy bitsy teeny weeny yellow dot bikini" can offer some shelter in a storm. Dummy has a diamond miniskirt. So pursue it as your only chance.

Dummy's top trumps are the only entries, so cherish and protect them. After winning the opening lead, play the ◇A and another diamond. The defenders may cash one heart and shift to trumps. Win in hand and lead another diamond.

Dummy's ♠K will win the next trump trick, but when both defenders follow to three diamonds and two hearts, you are home. Draw the last trump with dummy's ♠A, discard your low club on dummy's itsy bitsy, teeny weeny, yellow polka dot ◇2, and take the rest.

You did unblock dummy's ◇6, ◇7 and ◇9 on the first three rounds, didn't you? It's much more satisfying to win a trick with a nine than with a deuce.

DEAL 100. SEARCH AND YOU SHALL FIND

```
                    ♠ K 4
                    ♡ A K 3
                    ◇ 6 5 4 3 2
                    ♣ A K 4
♠ 9                                   ♠ 8 2
♡ Q 10 8 4                            ♡ J 9 5 2
◇ K J 10 9                            ◇ A Q 8 7
♣ Q J 10 6                            ♣ 9 8 3
                    ♠ A Q J 10 7 6 5 3
                    ♡ 7 6
                    ◇ void
                    ♣ 7 5 2
```

South opened 4♠. North had four aces and kings to show but only two levels of bidding space in which to cue-bid. Standard expert practice for responder after a 4♡ or 4♠ opening is to cue-bid the one outside suit in which you *don't* have an ace.

South was old enough to have learned that. Do today's bridge teachers still teach it?

Accordingly, North responded 5◇. With a diamond void, South bid 7♠.

West led the ♣Q. South counted his tricks twice. Still only 12. Desperation! "A girl's best friends may be diamonds," he thought, "but a declarer's best friends are defensive errors."

So that's what he played for, winning dummy's ♣K and running off all his trumps. West kept length behind dummy in the red suits. Declarer lost a club at the end. Down one.

North, a confirmed misogynist, said "Ugh, you play like a girl!"

Well, could a girl have made 7♠?

Yes. "Ooh, look at those gorgeous diamonds!" Any girl worth her salt would try to ruff them out, starting at Trick 2. With plenty of dummy entries and the suit splitting 4-4 ... a thirteenth trick.

DEAL 101. SHORT BUT SWEET

```
                    ♠ 10 5 4
                    ♡ J 9 7
                    ◇ 8 6 5
                    ♣ 10 9 4 3
      ♠ A 8 6 2                    ♠ K 9 7 3
      ♡ 6 5 4                      ♡ 8
      ◇ Q 10 4                     ◇ J 9 7 3 2
      ♣ K Q 8                      ♣ 7 6 5
                    ♠ Q J
                    ♡ A K Q 10 3 2
                    ◇ A K
                    ♣ A J 2
```

South opened an Omnibus 2♣, North "waited" with a neutral 2◇. South rebid 2♡ to show a game-forcing hand with primary hearts, North bid 2NT, the good-old-fashioned response to a Strong Two-Bid to show a very weak hand. South's 3♡ then showed a sixth heart, and still forced to bid something, North was happy enough to have three mediocre trumps and bid 4♡.

West made a passive trump lead.

"Ugh," said South when North spread the dummy. "Yarborough!"

"Not exactly," replied North, fingering her jack and two tens.

Grateful for those meager values, South won the first trick with dummy's ♡9 and let the ♣9 ride for a finesse. West won and continued trumps. This time dummy's ♡7 won the trick, enabling declarer to finesse the ♣J.

That too lost, and West exited with a third heart to dummy's ♡J. With the clubs blocked, declarer never got to use dummy's ♣10. Down one.

What powerful card in dummy did declarer overlook?

The other black ten, a *sure* tenth trick. Win the first heart in hand and lead the ♠Q. West can win and continue hearts. Win dummy's ♡9 and lead low towards the ♠J.

East can win and shift to either minor. Win in hand, cross to dummy's ♡J and discard the ♣2 on dummy's high ♠10. Ten tricks.

DEAL 102. BEAT THE DEVIL

```
                        ♠ Q 6 2
                        ♡ A
                        ◊ A J 7 6 3 2
                        ♣ Q 6 3              the Devil
        ♠ 10                                 ♠ 5 4
        ♡ K 10 5 4                           ♡ Q 9 8 7 3 2
        ◊ K Q 10 9 8                         ◊ 4
        ♣ J 9 4          Charlie             ♣ K 8 5 2
                        ♠ A K J 9 8 7 3
                        ♡ J 6
                        ◊ 5
                        ♣ A 10 7
```

After South's 1♠ opening and 3♠ jump rebid, North cue-bid twice and stopped in 6♠ when South could cue-bid only once.

South captured West's ◊K lead with dummy's ◊A. He saw a 75% chance to bring the club suit in with only one loser. After drawing trumps, he led the ♣7 to dummy's ♣Q, losing to the ♣K.

"That's one, Charlie," said the Devil.

Charlie won the heart return in dummy and led to his ♣10. West won the ♣J. "That's two, Charlie," said the Devil. "Two strikes and you're out!"

Poor Charlie replied, "I thought I get three strikes."

"You're not at Wrigley Field anymore, Charlie. Here you get only *two*."

What could *you* do with a third strike? Could you hit the ball out of the park?

Try diamonds, a second suit, first. It can't hurt. At Trick 2, ruff the ◊3 with the ♠7. Lead the ♠8 to dummy's ♠Q, noting the fall of the ♠10. Ruff the ◊6 with the ♠9. Lead the ♠3 to dummy's ♠6. Ruff the ◊7.

Enter dummy with the ♡A. Ruff the ◊J. Ruff the ♡J with dummy's ♠2. Discard the ♣7 on dummy's ◊2. You'll lose only a club at Trick 13.

The Devil will slink away, muttering "What the deuce! I think I'll go back to the O'Hell game."

DEAL 103. WELL HIDDEN

```
                    ♠ K J 5 3
                    ♡ A 4
                    ◊ A 10 6 3
                    ♣ J 9 3
    ♠ 9 7 4 2                       ♠ Q 10 8 6
    ♡ K 8 7 2                       ♡ J 10 9 6 5
    ◊ K 9 8                         ◊ Q 7 5
    ♣ 8 5                           ♣ 7
                    ♠ A
                    ♡ Q 3
                    ◊ J 4 2
                    ♣ A K Q 10 6 4 2
```

South opened 1♣ and jumped to 3♣ over North's 1◊ response. North's ♣4♣ raise, going beyond 3NT voluntarily, hinted at slam. When South took the hint by cue-bidding 4♠, North put him in 6♣.

West led a passive ♣5. Things looked grim for South. He saw only 11 top tricks and some face cards in the majors that didn't seem to be pulling full weight. He won in hand and cashed the ♠A.

He crossed to the ♣J to discard his heart loser on the ♠K and ruffed a spade, but the ♠Q did not fall. Twist and squirm, he could not avoid two diamond losers. Down one.

Unfriendly lie of the cards, or a poor effort. Want to try to make 6♣?

The title of this book provides a clue, of course. After winning the ♣A and ♣K, unblock the ♠A. Lead the ◊2 and cover West's card. That will see you home safely if West plays an honor or has both the ◊K and ◊Q.

However, East will capture dummy's ◊10 with the ◊Q and shift to the ♡J. Try the ♡Q, and capture West's ♡K with dummy's ♡A. Cash dummy's ◊A.

When the ◊K doesn't fall beneath it, discard your ◊J on dummy's ♠K, and ruff a diamond. When diamonds split 3-3, discard your low heart on dummy's fourth diamond and spread your hand.

DEAL 104. ANOTHER HIDDEN TREASURE

```
                    ♠ Q 8
                    ♡ A 9 7 5
                    ◊ A 8 6 2
                    ♣ A J 3
   ♠ J 10 6 5                        ♠ K 9 4 3 2
   ♡ Q J 6                           ♡ void
   ◊ Q 10 3                          ◊ J 9 5
   ♣ Q 9 5                           ♣ 10 8 6 4 2
                    ♠ A 7
                    ♡ K 10 8 4 3 2
                    ◊ K 7 4
                    ♣ K 7
```

North opened a 15-17 HCP 1NT and South jumped to 3♡, which they played as showing six hearts and slam hopes. North liked her three aces and four hearts. She jumped to 4♠, which they used as a keycard-ask with hearts trump. She bid 6♡ upon confirming that no key cards were missing.

West led the ♠J, covered all around. Bad news, as now South had possible fast spade loser. Two top hearts revealed a sure trump loser, more bad news. He cashed the ♣K, finessed the ♣J successfully, and pitched his spade loser on dummy's ♣A.

He ruffed a spade, cashed both top diamonds and threw West in with her trump trick, hoping she was out of diamonds and would have to surrender a ruff-and-sluff. No luck, down one.

"Nice try," said North consolingly. But could you make a nicer try still?

Yes, if you keep your eye on a hidden second suit, diamonds. To preserve an extra entry to the hand with the long (?) diamond, cash the ♡K at Trick 2. When East shows out, stop. Before drawing another trump, play on clubs: ♣K, finesse the ♣J (a necessary risk) and---uh uh uh uh, don't touch that spade!--- discard a *diamond* on the ♣A.

Now ◊K, ◊A, diamond ruff, and back to dummy's carefully-preserved ♡A. Presto change-o, your ♠7 disappears on dummy's ◊8. Making 6♡.

This time, we hope, partner's words of praise will be "My hero!"

DEAL 105. A GRAND PLAY

                    ♠ A 7 5 3
                    ♡ void
                    ◇ A Q J 10
                    ♣ 6 5 4 3 2
    ♠ 10 9   ♠ 2
    ♡ 10 8 6 3   ♡ Q 7 5 4 2
    ◇ 9 5 2   ◇ K 8 4 3
    ♣ K J 9 7   ♣ Q 10 8
                    ♠ K Q J 8 6 4
                    ♡ A K J 9
                    ◇ 7 6
                    ♣ A

South opened 1♠. North responded 4♡, a splinter, showing a forcing raise of spades with a heart singleton or void, in their partnership methods. Bad idea to use 4♡ and 4♠ jumps as artificial! South forgot, and bid 4NT, which they played as old-fashioned Blackwood. When North bid 5♡ in reply, South bid 7♡. North was puzzled, but had the good sense to correct to 7♠.

South won the opening spade lead and drew the last trump. He discarded two diamonds on his top hearts and ruffed the ♡0. When the ♡Q did not fall, he finesse the ◇Q. Down one. Not a strong effort.

Would you have found a superior line?

As usual, a long side suit in dummy offers extra chances. After winning Trick 1 in hand, unblock the ♣A. Cross to the ♠A and ruff a club. Cash both top hearts pitching diamonds from dummy and ruff the ♡9.

As before, the ♡Q doesn't fall, but when you ruff a second club and both defenders follow, you are home. Ruff the ♡J with dummy's last trump, ruff a third club, and now dummy's ◇A is the entry you need to throw your other diamond on dummy's fifth club. Were the clubs not 4-3, you could take a diamond finesse as a last resort

You need not know the percentages to compare this line to the line taken. This line works whenever the actual line does (if the ♡Q falls in the first three rounds, you don't need to rely on 4-3 clubs). Yet another deal where a second suit, even if headed by a six, provides an *extra* chance.

DEAL 106. WHAT ABOUT THE OTHER ONE?

```
                        ♠ 10 9 3
                        ♡ A K 9 8 6 4
                        ◊ 8 7 4 3
                        ♣ void
    ♠ 6 2                                 ♠ 7
    ♡ Q J 5 3                             ♡ 10 7 2
    ◊ J                                   ◊ K Q 10
    ♣ K Q J 9 5 4                         ♣ A 10 8 7 3 2
                        ♠ A K Q J 8 5 4
                        ♡ void
                        ◊ A 9 6 5 2
                        ♣ 6
```

South opened 1♠, but West's 2♣ overcall shut out the forcing 1NT response that North had contemplated. East's leap to 5♣, far from shutting South out, goaded him into bidding 6♠. As little as four low spades and a doubleton ◊K would make 6♠ a lock, and there was no bidding room left to make a slam try. Even 5◊ would simply suggest another place to play, and with three spades and four or five diamonds, North would pass.

South ruffed the ♣K lead in dummy, drew trump, and bet the house on 2-2 diamonds. Both defenders followed to the ◊A, but East won the next two tricks with the ◊KQ. Oops, down one.

Could you obtain more than the 40% chances of that declarer's line?

Yes. Why not try hearts? A 4-3 split will see you home. Ruff a heart high at Trick 2. Cross to the ♠9 and ruff another heart high. Cross to the ♠10 and throw two low diamonds on dummy's ♡AK.

When the missing heart honors come tumbling down, discard two more diamonds and claim.

Once again, a "can't cost, may gain" line. If the hearts don't split 4-3, you can still fall back on a 2-2 diamond split.

117

DEAL 107. LOTS OF QUESTIONS?

        ♠ J 10 3
        ♡ J 10 4
        ◊ K J 8 5 2
        ♣ A K

♠ Q 9 4 2   ♠ A 8 7 6
♡ K 6   ♡ 7 3
◊ 6 4   ◊ Q 10 9
♣ Q J 10 5 3   ♣ 9 8 6 2

        ♠ K 5
        ♡ A Q 9 8 5 2
        ◊ A 7 3
        ♣ 7 4

South opened 1♡ and enjoyed an uncontested auction to the obvious 4♡ game. Obvious, but not automatic, as two losers in spades and one loser in each red suit loomed.

After winning the opening club lead in dummy, declarer lost a trump finesse. He won the club return, finished trumps, cashed the ◊A and finessed dummy's ◊J. No luck there, either.

After winning the ◊Q, East led the ♠6, putting South to a guess. He guessed to play low. West won the ♠Q and returned a spade to East's ♠A. Down one.

How would you guess the spades?

Well, there's a clue: if West had the ♠A, he might have eked out a 2♣ overcall, so play East for the ♠A. But we posed a trick question. Why risk having to guess spades at all? Why finesse anything?

A brunette, a redhead and a blonde were discussing something---bananas, we suspect. The brunette said, "I like them long and thin." The redhead said, "I like them short and fat." We won't tell you what the blonde said, but they may as well have been talking about *second suits.* Though we'll stick with the brunette on bananas, we'll go with the redhead on *suits.*

Here the spades are short, fat and very sweet. Guess them however you like, but even after losing two spade tricks, you'll have set up a third on which to discard a diamond from your hand. You'll *make* 4♡ for sure.

DEAL 108. WHICH SECOND SUIT?

```
                    ♠ J 8 5
                    ♡ A K 7 5 2
                    ♢ A K 6 4 2
                    ♣ void
      ♠ A 6                            ♠ 7 3
      ♡ 9 4                            ♡ Q 10 8 3
      ♢ 10 9 8 7 3                     ♢ J
      ♣ A Q 8 7                        ♣ J 10 9 6 4 2
                    ♠ K Q 10 9 4 2
                    ♡ J 6
                    ♢ Q 5
                    ♣ K 5 3
```

North opened 1♡ and rebid 2♢ over South's 1♠, then raised South's 3♠ jump rebid to 6♠.

Anticipating that declarer may need to ruff clubs in dummy, West led the ♣A and continued with the ♣6.

Declarer counted 11 tricks. He needed to set up a trick in a red suit. But which? Diamonds or hearts?

South went for the diamonds because they were stronger. ♢Q, ♢K and oops---East showed out. Then he tried hearts: ♡K, ♡A, heart ruff and oops---West showed out.

South ruffed a club in dummy, threw another club on dummy's ♢A, and ruffed another heart, but---no way back to dummy to cash dummy's fifth heart. Losing the ♣A at Trick 13, and down one.

Just bad luck, or failure to think everything through?

When South had to choose which red suit to try, a 5-1 or 6-0 split in the suit he attacked could thwart him. As we saw, for lack of two dummy entries, he could not use dummy's hearts to recover from 5-1 diamonds.

But suppose he starts hearts first. Upon learning of a 5-1 (or 6-0) heart split, he can then try diamonds *where he needs only one dummy entry.* A club ruff with dummy's last trump provides it. (With a nod to Frank Stewart, who showed a similar theme some years ago).

119

DEAL 109. BARE-NAKED QUACKS

```
                    ♠ J 4 3
                    ♡ J 8 5
                    ◇ A Q 10
                    ♣ A Q 5 2
    ♠ 10 9 8 6                      ♠ Q 7 5 2
    ♡ K 6 2                         ♡ Q 10 9 4
    ◇ 7 3                           ◇ 5 2
    ♣ 10 9 8 3                      ♣ K 7 4
                    ♠ A K
                    ♡ A 7 3
                    ◇ K J 9 8 6 4
                    ♣ J 6
```

Auctions that start with a 2♣ response to 1◇ are trouble! Not so much for old-fashioned bidders, who play that opener's rebids (other than raises) beyond two of his first suit all promise extras and can thus rebid 2NT here, but severely for those who make non-jump 2NT rebids with minimums.

Thus South jump-rebid 3NT here. When North invited slam with 4NT, South recovered well by accepting with 6◇. North was happy to pass.

Fearing to lead from a king, West rejected a killer ♡2 opening lead in favor of a safe ♠10.

South won the ♠A. He drew trump and finessed the ♣Q, losing to the ♣K. East exited safely with the ♣7. On the run of the trumps, West clung to clubs and East clung to majors. 6◇ went down one.

Bad luck, or did South misplay?

Misplay. South took the wrong club finesse, the one that couldn't succeed even if it won. With AQxx facing Jx, and likewise AJxx facing Qx, the only finesse that can yield three tricks is low towards the doubleton quack.

It will succeed if a short king is in front of the quack, or a defender with a long king plays it on air ... as many Easts would here.

There are 1,594,323 suit combinations (including void opposite void) in the Naked City. You have seen 672 of them.

DEAL 110. HARD TO FIND

              ♠ A 2
              ♡ Q 9 3
              ◊ A J 10 5
              ♣ 7 5 4 2

♠ K 7 6 3   ♠ J 10 9 5 4
♡ 7 2   ♡ 5
◊ K Q 7 4   ◊ 9 8 6 3 2
♣ K 10 8   ♣ J 9

              ♠ Q 8
              ♡ A K J 10 8 6 4
              ◊ ----
              ♣ A Q 6 3

South opened 1♡. West doubled for takeout, and North redoubled to show a stronger-than-average hand. Taking advantage of favorable probability, East jumped to 3♠ preemptively.

When South bid 4♡, North cue-bid 4♠ to show the ♠A and interest in a heart slam. That was enough for South to gamble 6♡.

Perhaps a passive trump lead would have been better, but West led the ◊ K.

Declarer discarded the ♣3 on dummy's ◊A and continued with the ◊J to discard the ♣6. West won the ◊Q and exited in trump. South drew trumps, discarded the ♠8 on dummy's ◊10 and finessed the ♣Q.

No surprise, West won the ♣K. Down one.

Could you take better advantage of West's unwittingly helpful lead?

Second suit? Perhaps not exactly. Dummy's clubs also offer *side-suit potential*. After winning West's trump exit at Trick 3, unblock the ♣A, lead low to dummy's ♡9 to draw the last trump, and discard the ♣Q on dummy's ◊10.

Now ruff a club, cross to the ♠A and ruff another club. Cross to dummy's ♠A, discard your ♠Q on dummy's ♣7, and claim.

Was it Gloria Kleinem who said, "Sometimes the best second suit for a job is a third suit!"?

121

CHAPTER 8
A Little Of This, A Lot Of That

DEAL 111. WHICH ROAD TO TRAVEL?

                          ♠ 7 4 3 2
                          ♡ A K 8 5 4
                          ◊ Q J
                          ♣ 3 2
        ♠ 9   ♠ 6 5
        ♡ J 10 7 6   ♡ Q
        ◊ 10 9 7 6   ◊ 8 5 4 3 2
        ♣ K 10 8 6   ♣ J 9 7 5 4
                          ♠ A K Q J 10 8
                          ♡ 9 3 2
                          ◊ A K
                          ♣ A Q

After a strong, artificial and forcing 2♣ opening and a natural positive 2♡ response, South rebid 2♠ and North raised to 3♠. Roman Keycard Blackwood followed promptly. When North could do no more than show the ♡K in reply to his Specific King Ask, South stopped in 6♠.

West's ◊10 opening lead rode to South's ◊A. South drew trump, and with nary an entry to dummy outside of hearts, he decided to duck a heart to preserve the entry that could enable him to run the suit. If hearts split badly, he could fall back on a club finesse as a last resort.

Before tackling hearts, however, South took the ◊K, in case a foolish defender might give him a ruff-and-sluff. Then he deep-finessed the ♡8 in case a foolish West might fail to split three honors. East won the ♡Q and led the ◊5. Finesse or play for 3-2 hearts? He chose the latter. Down one.

"Nice try," said North sweetly. Could you have found a nicer try?

Duck a heart, but on the second round, not the first. Lead low to dummy's ♡K and back to your ♡9. You will discover a 4-1 heart split before you must guess what to do on a club shift. When East has a singleton heart honor, a third-round finesse against West will bring home the hearts for four tricks and a needed club discard.

Thanks to Eddie Kantar, Mr. Take-All-Your-Chances himself, for this neat deal that also illustrates how to play another 30 suit combinations

DEAL 112. THE DEVIL PULLS A FAST ONE

                          ♠ 2
                          ♡ A Q 3 2
                          ◊ A Q 10 8 7 6
    the Devil   ♣ A 4
    ♠ Q 10 8 7 4   ♠ K J
    ♡ 4   ♡ 8 5
    ◊ 9 2   ◊ K J 4 3
    ♣ K J 10 8 6   ♣ Q 9 7 5 2
                          ♠ A 9 6 5 3
                          ♡ K J 10 9 7 6
                          ◊ 5
                          ♣ 3

When South responded 1♡ to North's 1◊ opening, North's hand became enormous, worth a force to game. Though a 4◊ jump was also available to show a 6-4 game raise, North chose a 3♠ splinter, showing a singleton or void. South's "Kickback" 4♠ asked for keys in hearts, and North's 4NT reply showed the three missing aces. South gambled 7♡.

South won the trump lead in hand. Which side suit to try to ruff out? He chose spades---"Because it's *mine!*" he explained in the post-mortem.

So, ♠A, spade ruff. ◊A, diamond ruff. Spade ruff with dummy's ♡Q and ... East discards the ♣2.

"Curses, foiled again!' muttered South.

"Don't steal my lines," objected the Devil, who was sitting West. "Just give me a spade at the end, and you'll get off cheap for down one."

"You won't even ask for my soul, Mr. Mephistopheles?" said South. When the Devil shook his head no, South continued, "Deal!" and threw his cards in. Did South do right?

No. How could it ever be right to make a deal with the Devil?

Upon seeing spades split 5-2, South can ruff a second diamond high, cross to the ♡A to finish trumps, and ruff a third diamond. Then lead to dummy's ♣A and discard spades on dummy's diamonds. Making 7♡.

DEAL 113. AN UNUSUAL DISCARD

```
              ♠ A K 8 6 4 3
              ♡ Q 9 2
              ◊ 6 2
              ♣ A 2
♠ Q 10 7 5                      ♠ J
♡ 6                            ♡ 8 5 3
◊ K 9 5 4                      ◊ 8 7 3
♣ J 10 9 3                     ♣ Q 8 7 6 5 4
              ♠ 9 2
              ♡ A K J 10 7 4
              ◊ A Q J 10
              ♣ K
```

After a 1♠ response to 1♡ and a 3◊ jump shift, North drove to 7♡.

South won West 's ♣J opening lead with his ♣K. He'd had bad luck with finesses before, so he thought to avoid a diamond finesse here. He saw one diamond discard coming on dummy's ♣A and thought to set up dummy's spades for two more.

Aware of the need to preserve dummy entries, South cashed only the ♡A and led to dummy's ♡9, saving dummy's ♡Q as a late entry to run the spades after ruffing them out. Hoping for 3-2 spades, he cashed the ♠AK.

Did we say "cashed"? Sorry. East ruffed and shifted to the ◊8. Too late now for anything but a finesse. West captured the ◊Q with his ◊K. Down two.

"Tough luck," said North sympathetically. "A five-or-seven deal."

Was she right?

Not quite. It was a *seven*-or-seven deal. After cashing the ♡A, lead to the ♠K, *shed a spade on dummy's ♣A*, and ruff a spade high. Cross to the ♡9 and ruff another spade high.
Finish trumps with a heart to dummy's ♡Q, and now the spades run for the three diamond discards desired.

DEAL 114. THE DEVIL MAKES A SWEET DEAL

```
                    ♠ K J 8 2
                    ♡ A Q J 8
                    ◊ J 7 2
                    ♣ K 2                the Devil
        ♠ 7                              ♠ 10 6 5 4
        ♡ 7 5 4                          ♡ 10 6 3
        ◊ A K 8 6 4                      ◊ Q 10 9 5
        ♣ Q 10 9 4                       ♣ 7 5
                    ♠ A Q 9 3
                    ♡ K 9 2
                    ◊ 3
                    ♣ A J 8 6 3
```

West's 1◊ overcall gave North a chance to show both majors at once with a Negative Double, the only one that promises both majors. South made a great rebid, a 3♠ jump that showed the full value of his hand. North cue-bid 4♣, a cue bid of partner's first suit being perfectly fine with either the ace or king. South checked for key cards with a Roman Keycard Blackwood 4NT and bid 6♠ over the 5♡ reply. A fine aggressive auction!

West led and continued diamonds. South ruffed the second and tried to ruff out clubs, his five-card side suit. Declarer cashed two rounds of spades, then tried to set up his second suit, clubs.

But a gleeful East overruffed the third club and exited with his last trump. Down two, as East score the ◊Q later.

North looked to her left and noticed her opponent's horns and tail. "You dirty Devil!" she cried. "How dare you overruff *me*?"

East replied: "I normally take the souls of people like you, but I'll spare yours if you'll do me a small favor. Two charlatans, 'Dr J' and 'Mister Spots' are writing a book on 'Second Suits' that slanders me. Warn your friends against buying it. Do you see the harm those two did here?

They took a simple dummy reversal and turned it into a second suit fiasco. At Trick Three, just cash the ace and queen of spades, cross to dummy, ruff the ◊J with your last trump, cross to dummy, finish trumps and claim."

Thank you, Mr. Mephistopheles. All publicity is good publicity.

DEAL 115. WHERE TO WIN?

                          ♠ A Q 5
                          ♡ Q 5
                          ◊ 7 3
                          ♣ K J 9 6 4 2

    ♠ J 10   ♠ 9 8 4 3
    ♡ 10 3   ♡ 8 6 2
    ◊ A K Q 10 8 2   ◊ J 6 4
    ♣ 10 8 3   ♣ A Q 7

                          ♠ K 7 6 2
                          ♡ A K J 9 7 4
                          ◊ 9 5
                          ♣ 5

South opened 1♡ and West overcalled 2◊. North forced with 3♣. Strapped for a rebid over South's 3♡, he chose 4♡ as the least of evils.

West led the ◊K and cashed the ◊A next, then shifted to the ♠J. Declarer won in the short hand with dummy's ♠A and drew trump, discarding a club from dummy.

Then he finessed dummy's ♣J, hoping West had the ♣Q, but East won it and tapped declarer with the ◊J. Declarer led to dummy's ♠Q and back to his ♠K, hoping for a 3-3 spade split.

Not today: down one.

Can you improve upon declarer's play? What deal type is this? Hint: what's the theme of this book?

Trick hint! You might play for 3-3 clubs and try to ruff the suit out, preserving dummy's ♠A and ♠Q at entries. We like it and it will work.

But declarer missed a second chance. Don't you recognize a simple squeeze when you see one? After losing a club finesse and ruffing East's last diamond, you can run off the rest of the trumps. If the spades split 3-3 or the ♣A is with the long spades, the spades will run or the holder of the fourth spade will be squeezed out of it. Much more fun!

DEAL 116. DANGER LURKING

```
                    ♠ 7 4
                    ♡ A 9
                    ◊ Q 10 2
                    ♣ A 9 8 7 6 5
    ♠ A 6 5                        ♠ Q J 10 9
    ♡ K Q J 10 8                   ♡ 7 5 4 3 2
    ◊ 7 5 3                        ◊ 6
    ♣ 10 4                         ♣ K Q J
                    ♠ K 8 3 2
                    ♡ 6
                    ◊ A K J 9 8 4
                    ♣ 3 2
```

After South opened 1◊, West's 1♡ overcall posed a terrible problem for North. His hand was slightly too weak for 2♣ and his suit was slightly too weak for 3♣, which his partnership played as invitational. He compromised with 2◊, figuring that by limiting his hand early, he could then bid clubs later.

"Later" never came, as East jumped to 4♡ and South bid 5◊ as a sacrifice, escaping undoubled.

West led the ♡K. Declarer won dummy's ♡A and planned the play. He recognized a "second suit" deal. To prepare to ruff out the clubs, he led a low club from dummy as Trick 2.

East won the ♣J but refrained from continuing hearts. Instead he shifted to the ♠Q. South went down one quickly.

"Great save!" said North. "We can't beat 4♡."

Well, was it a "great save"?

No, it was a botched "second suit" *make*. Southeast, a kibitzer, turned to his kibitzee and said, "Haven't you read Jim and Danny's 'Lots Of Laughs' book?

Just let West win the king of hearts. Then you can pitch a club on the ace of hearts and keep that dangerous East out. You'll be able to ruff out the clubs in peace."

We think he meant our *Loser on Loser* book.

DEAL 117. SNEAKY, SNEAKY

                          ♠ K J 10 5 3
                          ♡ 4 2
                          ◊ 9 5 4
                          ♣ 9 5 3
        ♠ 7 4 2   ♠ 9 6
        ♡ Q J 10   ♡ 9 8 7 6 3
        ◊ K 7 6 3   ◊ A Q 2
        ♣ 8 6 2   ♣ Q J 10
                          ♠ A Q 8
                          ♡ A K 5
                          ◊ J 10 8
                          ♣ A K 7 4

South opened 2NT and accepted North's 3♡ Jacoby Transfer, then chose 4♠ when North rebid 3NT to offer a choice of games.

When he saw the dummy, South said, "Sorry, pard. Maybe I should have passed three notrump."

Perhaps. If the diamonds split 4-3, or the suit blocks, or West leads some other suit, 3NT rolls.

In 4♠, South won the ♡A and drew trump. When he ducked a club next, East won and knew just what to do. East shifted to the ◊Q and the defense took three diamond trick. Down one.

Is there a way to make 4♠?

Maybe. Duck the opening lead nonchalantly. If West continues hearts, discard the ♣3 on a heart winner.

Two top clubs and a club ruff will see you home if clubs split 3-3 and spades 3-2, as your fourth club will become your tenth trick.

DEAL 118. THE DEVIL'S MULLIGAN

```
                      ♠ J 6
                      ♡ A 5 4 2
                      ◇ A
                      ♣ A K 8 7 3 2      the Devil
      ♠ 10 8 5 4                         ♠ 9 3
      ♡ Q 9                              ♡ J 10 8 3
      ◇ K Q J 5 4                        ◇ 10 9 7
      ♣ 9 4                              ♣ Q J 10 6
                      ♠ A K Q 7 2
                      ♡ K 7 6
                      ◇ 8 6 3 2
                      ♣ 5
```

Lots of high cards without an eight-card fit seduced North-South to reach 6♠ via an auction we dare not repeat lest a seven-year-old child see this book on Mommy's coffee table and take its bidding as exemplary.

West led the ◇K to dummy's ◇A, Seeing only 10 tricks, declarer envisioned dummy's clubs as a source for two more and started clubs promptly. ♣K, club ruff; ♠J and three more spades to finish trumps, throwing hearts from dummy. Heart to the ♡A, ♣A and pray for the two remaining clubs to fall together. When they didn't---down two.

The game this evening had started early. East looked at his watch and smiled when he saw his favorite time, 6:66 PM.

"Ah, the Magical Mulligan Minute!" said East. "Any takers? Special price if you act now, just a 666-year lease on your soul if you fail again. I'd hate to tell you the regular price. If you have to ask, you can't afford it."

Would you take Mr. Mephistopheles up on his merciful offer, dear reader? If so, how would you play 6♠ after the same opening lead?

Return kindness for kindness. Lead the ♣2 from dummy at Trick 2. East can win and shift to the ♡J, but you'll win the ♡K, cross to the ♠J and ruff a low club. Finish trumps, cross to the ♡A, and run clubs for the rest.

The Devil will slink away muttering "What the deuce!"

131

DEAL 119. HIGH AND HIGH AGAIN

                        ♠ A Q 5 3
                        ♡ 8 6 3
                        ◊ A 10 5 3
                        ♣ 10 2
    ♠ 6   ♠ J 8 4
    ♡ Q J 10 5 4   ♡ A K 9 7
    ◊ J 8 4   ◊ K Q 7 6
    ♣ Q 9 4 3   ♣ K 6
                        ♠ K 10 9 7 2
                        ♡ 2
                        ◊ 9 2
                        ♣ A J 8 7 5

North and South were playing *Hamilton*, a comprehensive notrump defense in which 2♡ or 2♠ shows that major and an unspecified minor. East opened 1NT and South overcalled 2♠.

West countered with another popular convention, Lebensohl; his 2NT showed a hand strong enough to compete at the three-level but too weak to force to game ... or some other kind of hand that varies from one version of Lebensohl to another. Danny says no convention too complex to explain should be legal, and he's never heard Lebensohl explained correctly.

No matter, North jumped to 4♠, perhaps to make, perhaps to sacrifice against a not-yet-found 4♡ game. West led the ♡Q against 4♠.

South ruffed the second heart. He played the ♣A and another club. East won and continued hearts. South ruffed, and ruffed a club with the ♠Q.

He reentered his hand with the ♠K and ruffed another club with the ♠A. But now East's ♠J scored. South lost one trick in each suit. Down one.

A hard contract to make, but do you see a way?

With some good card reading, yes. As you may need to ruff clubs high in dummy, play the 1NT opener for the ♠J. Duck a club at Trick 3, ruff the next heart, then ♣A, club ruff high, finesse your ♠10, club ruff high, and finesse your ♠10 to pick up trumps, your fifth club, and the ◊A. Ten tricks.

DEAL 120. ASSURING YOUR CONTRACT

                         ♠ 5
                         ♡ A Q J 4 3 2
                         ◇ 8 6 3
                         ♣ A J 5
        ♠ K J 6 3   ♠ A 10 8 7 2
        ♡ 10 9 8 7 5   ♡ 6
        ◇ K Q 10   ◇ 9 5 4 2
        ♣ 4   ♣ 8 3 2
                         ♠ Q 9 4
                         ♡ K
                         ◇ A J 7
                         ♣ K Q 10 9 7 6

After South's game-forcing 2♣ response to 1♡ and his 3♣ rebid over North's 2♡, North showed club support, slam hopes and a singleton or void in spades with a 4♠ splinter. East doubled to suggest a spade sacrifice.

Having both the ◇A and the filling ♡K in partner's suit, South bid 6♣. West thought of sacrificing in 6♠ but with both diamond strength and enough hearts to keep dummy's hearts from running he saw hope of beating 6♣, so he refrained.

Despite East's double of the 4♠ splinter, West led the ◇K. Envisioning 13 tricks, South won, cashed the ♣K and ♣A, and unblocked the ♡K. He led to dummy's ♣J, drawing the last trump, and played dummy's hearts from the top, discarding all three spades, the ◇7 and then ...

Oops, "then" never came: West won the fifth heart and cashed the ◇Q. Down one.

Was there no prophylactic against a 5-1 heart split?

There was. After cashing the ♣K, unblock the ♡K. Then cross to dummy's ♣A and ruff a low heart high. The ♣J remains as an entry to dummy, and dummy's four remaining hearts let declarer discard three spades and a diamond: 12 tricks.

But there is no prophylactic against overtrick greed.

DEAL 120. ANOTHER SELF-EXECUTION

```
                    ♠ A 5 4 2
                    ♡ Q J 7 4 2
                    ◇ A K
                    ♣ K 5
   ♠ 10 9 8 7                      ♠ 6
   ♡ A K                           ♡ 10 9 8 6
   ◇ Q 10 3                        ◇ J 4
   ♣ A J 7 2                       ♣ Q 10 9 8 6 4
                    ♠ K Q J 3
                    ♡ 5 3
                    ◇ 9 8 7 6 5 2
                    ♣ 3
```

After West opened 1♣ on favorable vulnerability, North doubled for takeout with a hand good enough to bid hearts over South's possible diamond bid. East bid 3♣, which in standard methods is a weak jump raise over an intervening double, and South joined the fray with an aggressive (misnamed) "responsive" double to show "at least two places to play."

Having extras, North jumped to 4♡ and South's 4♠ ended the auction.

West led the ♠ 10, which declarer let ride to his ♠K. He cashed the ◇AK and came to his hand with the ♠Q. East discarded. Trouble brewing!

West covered the third diamond, and now declarer had to ruff with dummy's ♠A to preserve a trump entry to his hand. He led to his ♠J but now West ruffed the next diamond with the master trump and cashed the ♣A and ♡AK to beat 4♠.

"Which side are you on?" sang North. Why was he asking?

Declarer slipped at Trick 1 by wasting an entry to the hand he intended to make the *master hand*. Look how the deal plays out if he wins Trick 1 with dummy's ♠A.
◇AK, low to the ♠K. Diamond ruff in dummy, low to the ♠Q. The ♠J to pull West's last trump, and then three long diamonds. Ten tricks before catching your breath.

It's the *other side's* job to remove entries to your long suit, not yours

134

DEAL 122. MAINTAINING CONTROL

```
                    ♠ Q 10 5
                    ♡ K 6 3
                    ◇ A
                    ♣ A K 9 5 3 2
  ♠ 9 8 7 3                              ♠ J
  ♡ Q J 10 9                            ♡ 8 7 2
  ◇ Q 3 2                               ◇ K 10 8 5 4
  ♣ J 6                                 ♣ Q 10 8 4
                    ♠ A K 6 4 2
                    ♡ A 5 4
                    ◇ J 9 7 6
                    ♣ 7
```

South responded 1♠ to North's 1♣ opening, and forced again with 3♡ over North's 3♣ jump. With a hand that grew and grew, North jumped again, and over his 4♠ South bid 6♠. Well bid!

West led the ♡Q. Declarer won the ♡A and drew trump. Dummy's ♣AK provided a diamond discard, and declarer ruffed a club. But he ruffed with his last trump.

However, that was only 10 tricks. Dummy's fifth and sixth clubs rotted on the vine. Down two.

Where did South go wrong? Could you have kept control and scored dummy's fifth and six hearts?

Yes, if instead of ruffing the third club, you'd discarded. Win East's red-suit return in dummy and ruff the fourth club.

Then return to dummy in the other red suit to take another two tricks with dummy's long clubs.

DEAL 123. PERCENTAGES

```
                    ♠ K 7 5 4 2
                    ♡ J 4
                    ◊ A J 10 8
                    ♣ 10 4
    ♠ 9 8                              ♠ Q 10 6 3
    ♡ K Q 10 7 3                       ♡ A 8 6 5
    ◊ 6 3                              ◊ 4
    ♣ Q 8 6 2                          ♣ K 9 7 5
                    ♠ A J
                    ♡ 9 2
                    ◊ K Q 9 7 5 2
                    ♣ A J 3
```

South opened 1◊ and eked out a 3◊ jump over North's 1♠ response. North bid 4◊ to accept game while offering a chance for South to bid a likely easier 4♠ game with three-card support, but South had nothing better to do but bid 5◊.

West led the ♡K against 5◊ and continued the ♡Q, then shifted to the ♣2. South captured East's ♣K with the ♣A and needed two discards for his other two clubs.

He drew trump and tried to ruff out the spades, needing a 3-3 split. No luck, down one.

Could you do better?

Maybe. A 3-3 split is a 36% chance and a 4-2 split is a 48% chance. That's a combined 84%. Half of that 84% of the time, or 42% of the time, East will have the ♠Q.

Thus finessing East for the ♠Q offers a 6% higher chance than trying for a 3-3 split. If it works, you will be able to throw both your remaining clubs, on dummy's ♠K and dummy's fifth spade.

Actually, the gain from finessing is greater than 6%. The play thus far suggests that West started with ♡KQxxx and ♣Qxxx. Don't you think he might have intervened over 1◊ if he had ♠Qxx as well?

If you needed only one discard from dummy's spades, you'd do well to ruff them out, but needing two discards you'll do better to finesse.

DEAL 124. CAREFUL DISCARDING

                    ♠ J 9 5
                    ♡ Q 10 5 3
                    ◇ 7 6 5 3 2
                    ♣ A

♠ Q 10   ♠ K 7 6 4 3 2
♡ 7   ♡ 6
◇ J 9 8 4   ◇ void
♣ K Q J 8 6 4   ♣ 10 9 7 5 3 2

                    ♠ A 8
                    ♡ A K J 9 8 4 2
                    ◇ A K Q 10
                    ♣ void

One hazard of the Omnibus 2♣ opening is opposing preemption before you get to tell your story. Old-timers who followed the advice of Culbertson and Goren used Strong Two-Bids, largely avoiding that hazard.

West's 3♣ overcall of South's Omnibus 2♣ was not "Michaels"; it showed clubs. East was on the ball. Not knowing what species of "moose" South had, he took a "premature save" in 7♣. The expletive that South uttered is not printable here, but he was goaded into bidding 7♡.

Everyone passed. West led the ♣K. South showed his hand, claiming 13 tricks. West demurred: "Down one. You lose a diamond in the end."

Well, who was right? Did South have a valid claim?

Yes, if he'd said, "Discarding the ten of diamonds, cashing my two top hearts then my diamonds, leading a heart to dummy to ruff a diamond, and another heart to dummy to pitch my low spade on dummy's last diamond."

Without such a statement, South must be presumed to throw the ♠8 carelessly on dummy's ♣A, and go down.

West shook a finger at East. "Don't we still use Lightner Doubles? You should have doubled. How else could I guess to lead diamonds?"

DEAL 125. OPTIMIST OR PESSIMIST?

```
                        ♠ 8 7 6
                        ♡ A 10 8
                        ◊ 8
                        ♣ A K Q J 3 2
        ♠ K Q 5                         ♠ 10 9 4 3 2
        ♡ 5 3 2                         ♡ 6
        ◊ A Q J 10 9 7                  ◊ K 4
        ♣ 10                            ♣ 9 7 6 5 4
                        ♠ A J
                        ♡ K Q J 9 7 4
                        ◊ 6 5 3 2
                        ♣ 8
```

South opened 1♡. West overcalled 2◊, and North bid 3♣, forcing to game even among those two do not play Two-Over-One Game-Forcing. After South rebid 3♡, North cue-bid 4◊, showing good three-card heart support and some slam hope. Having strong hearts, South cooperated with a 4♠ cue bid of his own. With second-round diamond control and a splendid source of tricks, North ventured 6♡.

When West led the ♠K instead of the expected diamond and South saw the dummy, he said, "Nice hand. Maybe we missed seven."

"Don't make eight," said North. "Be happy enough to make six. In the other room, they'll probably stop in game." (They were playing teams.)

South won the ♠A, drew trump and said, "Thirteen tricks," showing his hand. "Down one," said East, showing her clubs. "I knew it," said North.

What did South forget?

The Prudent Pessimist Question, "What can go wrong?" A 5-1 split occurs about one time in seven. Take extra care when you're in six.

Win the ♠A and cash only the ♡ KQ, then take the ♣A and ruff a club high. Draw the last trump with dummy's ♡A. Run clubs for 12 tricks.

You don't need 13.

DEAL 126. THE MARK OF AN EXPERT

$\spadesuit$ A Q 9
$\heartsuit$ 8 7 6 5 2
$\diamond$ A 10 7
$\clubsuit$ K 8

$\spadesuit$ 6 4 2 $\spadesuit$ void
$\heartsuit$ A 10 9 3 $\heartsuit$ K J 4
$\diamond$ 5 2 $\diamond$ J 9 8 6
$\clubsuit$ Q J 10 4 $\clubsuit$ A 9 7 6 5 3

$\spadesuit$ K J 10 8 7 5 3
$\heartsuit$ Q
$\diamond$ K Q 4 3
$\clubsuit$ 2

Competition in clubs pushed South to 5$\spadesuit$ on adverse vulnerability. West led the $\clubsuit$Q, covered by the $\clubsuit$K ("just in case"). East won the $\clubsuit$A and returned the $\clubsuit$6.

South ruffed, drew trump and played on diamonds. The defense scored a heart and a diamond. Down one.

Unlucky, 3-0 trumps and 4-2 diamonds. An insurmountable obstacle?

Frank Stewart asks "What separates a good player from an expert?" He answers, "A good player practices till he gets it right. An expert practices till he never gets it wrong."

Did you see the extra chance that South missed?

Lead the $\heartsuit$Q to Trick 3. Some day, both defenders will duck. They say it happened to old-time expert Harry Harkavy regularly. But suppose West wins and leads a trump. Win in dummy and ruff a heart high. Lead a trump to dummy and ruff another heart high.

Hallelujah, both defenders still follow. A third trump to dummy and a third heart ruff. Your fourth diamond goes on dummy's fifth heart.

Even a caddy---Jim's golf caddy, that is---could make 5$\spadesuit$ when diamonds split 3-3. An expert declarer makes 5$\spadesuit$ when they don't.

DEAL 127. RIGHT IDEA

```
                    ♠ K Q
                    ♡ A 10
                    ◊ K 9 6 4 2
                    ♣ A K 4 3
   ♠ 9                              ♠ J 5 3
   ♡ K 9 5 2                        ♡ Q 8 6 4
   ◊ Q 10 8 7                       ◊ 5
   ♣ J 10 9 2                       ♣ Q 8 7 6 5
                    ♠ A 10 8 7 6 4 2
                    ♡ J 7 3
                    ◊ A J 3
                    ♣ void
```

South responded 1♠ to North's 1◊ opening, and rebid 3♠ over North's 3♣ jump shift. North raised to 4♠. Then a 5◊ cue bid, a 5♡ cue bid and a "Josephine" 5NT (begging for a grand slam with strong trumps) fetched a jump to 7♠ from North.

West led a "safe" ♣J. South threw the ◊3 on dummy's ♣K, unblocked dummy's ♠KQ, came to his hand with the ◊A and drew the last trump. He led the ◊J to West's ◊Q and dummy's ◊K.

A 3-2 split would let him ruff out the diamonds and cross to dummy's ♡A to cash all the tricks he needed. But the 4-1 diamond split left him with a heart loser. Down one.

Could you overcome that 4-1 split?

Yes, by ruffing two diamonds to set up the one extra diamond trick you need. Discard *two* diamonds promptly on dummy's ♣AK. Unblock the ◊A. Cross to dummy twice with dummy's two royal trumps to ruff two low diamonds in hand.

Draw the last trump with your ♠A, and cross to dummy's ♡A. Now you can discard both your remaining hearts on the ◊K and dummy's fifth diamond.

An interesting deal! Did anyone ever tell you, "Always lead safely against a grand slam!"? Would you ever consider leading from king-fourth? But here a ♡2 lead, *attacking an entry to dummy's long suit*, beats 7♠.

DEAL 128. STOP COMPLAINING

```
                        ♠ 7 6 5
                        ♡ A Q 7 5 3 2
                        ◊ 8
                        ♣ A Q 4
        ♠ 8 3 2                        ♠ 4
        ♡ 8 4                          ♡ K J 10 9
        ◊ K J 5 4                      ◊ A Q 10 6
        ♣ J 9 6 3                      ♣ 10 8 7 2
                        ♠ A K Q J 10 9
                        ♡ 6
                        ◊ 9 7 3 2
                        ♣ K 5
```

Some devotees of 2/1 GF cite as its main selling point the "slow" auctions to game that supposedly ease the path to slam. Here North and South were playing SOFA (Standard Old-Fashioned American). After responding 2♡ to South's 1♠ opening, North could not yet tell the right strain for game and could force only by bidding a new suit. She chose 3♣. Bravo!

North's 3♣ turned South's ♣K into a proven value, so he jumped to 4♠ to show a solid suit in a hand improved by the 3♣ bid. Bravo!

South gambled 6♠, thinking that at worst it hinged on a heart finesse.

West might have led diamonds, the unbid suit, against 6♠, but sniffing a singleton diamond, he led an annoying ♠3.

South won and led the ◊3, but West won the ◊J and led the ♠2. Now declarer counted only 11 tricks. He fell back on a heart finesse as his last resort. East won the ♡K. A fast down one.

"Without the trump lead, I'd have made it," griped South.

"A bit more thought would let you make it too," said North. Could he?

Yes, with Plan B, setting up a second suit. ♡A, heart ruff. Diamond to West, another trump. Diamond ruff, heart ruff, ♣Q, heart ruff. ♠A throwing a club from dummy, and with ♡Q7 ♣A left, dummy is high. Making 6♠.

DEAL 129. TANGLED UP

```
                    ♠ A K 8
                    ♡ A K 9 8 7 6
                    ◊ Q 6
                    ♣ A Q
    ♠ J 6 5                         ♠ 10
    ♡ 10 4                          ♡ Q J 3 2
    ◊ J 9 2                         ◊ K 10 4
    ♣ J 9 7 6 3                     ♣ K 10 5 4 2
                    ♠ Q 9 7 4 3 2
                    ♡ 5
                    ◊ A 8 7 5 3
                    ♣ 8
```

North opened an Omnibus 2♣ and rebid 2♡ over South's neutral 2◊ response. South now bid a natural positive 2♠ and North raised to 3♠. South's 4◊ cue bid let North use Roman Keycard Blackwood. North settled for 6♠ when South denied any minor-suit king.

Declarer won West's ♣6 opening lead with dummy's ♣A, sensibly declining to finesse. He cashed dummy's ♡K and ruffed a heart, took the ♠Q and led to dummy's ♠K. When he ruffed another heart, however, West overruffed with the ♠J.

South ruffed the club return, but three diamond discards on dummy's remaining ♡A98 were one too few. Down one.

It would seem six trump tricks, four heart tricks, and two minor-suit aces should produce the needed 12 tricks, but somehow they got tangled up. Do you see how to untangle them without risking a heart overruff?

As you have 12 tricks, you can afford to lose one. You may as well lose a heart trick as a trick elsewhere. So lose it … at Trick 3. Cash the ♠Q and duck a heart. The defender who wins may tap you in clubs, but you'll ruff, lead to the ♠K, and ruff a heart on the *second* round of the suit when both defenders must still follow.

A trump to dummy's ♠A draws the last trump, and now dummy's four heart tricks provide discards for your four low diamonds.

Simple but elusive!

DEAL 130. DON'T GO DOWN QUICKLY

```
              ♠ 7 5
              ♡ Q J 8 6 2
              ◊ K 8 6 4 2
              ♣ 6
♠ K 9 4                        ♠ 10 8 6 3 2
♡ 7 4                          ♡ 5
◊ A 9 5 3                      ◊ Q J 10
♣ Q 9 8 3                      ♣ K 10 5 2
              ♠ A Q J
              ♡ A K 10 9 3
              ◊ 7
              ♣ A J 7 4
```

South opened 1♡ and North bid a "Weak Freak" 4♡. Visualizing a finesse for 6♡ opposite as little as queen-fifth in each red suit, South bid it.

West led the ♡4. South won. "May as well get it over quickly," she thought. "If we can get another chukker in before the club closes tonight, I can earn next month's rent as well as this month's." So she drew the last trump with dummy's ♡J and took a spade finesse. Down one.

Sure, swift, and wrong. Need we add that she did get another chukker in but lost that one too?

Do you see how she could have saved at least one month's rent?

With a choice of two possible lines, take the one that won't put you down immediately if it fails.

You cannot yet tell if this is a "finesse" deal or a "second suit" deal. The finesse will put you down immediately if it fails. Trying to set up a second suit keeps you "in the game" to take a finesse later.

So, cash a second trump in hand and lead the ◊7. If West has the ◊A, he may duck (one chance). If West grabs the ◊A, a 4-3 diamond split will let you ruff the suit out and discard two spades (another chance).

If all else fails, a "last resort" spade finesse provides a third chance. Three chances are better than one.

DEAL 131. 50%, 75%, OR 100%?

```
                    ♠ A Q J 10 9
                    ♡ Q 9 7 3
                    ◊ 10 2
                    ♣ A Q
   ♠ K 5 3 2                          ♠ 8 6 4
   ♡ 8 2                              ♡ 4
   ◊ K 7 6                            ◊ 8 5 4 3
   ♣ J 10 9 8                         ♣ K 7 6 4 2
                    ♠ 7
                    ♡ A K J 10 6 5
                    ◊ A Q J 9
                    ♣ 5 3
```

North and South used Jacoby Forcing Raises. North's 2NT response showed a balanced forcing heart raise. South was required to show "shortness" if any; his 3♠ showed a singleton or void in spades. Then 4♣, 4◊ and (as they used a "Kickback" 4♠ to ask for keys in hearts) 4NT cue bids showed all three side aces. Lacking any side king to show, South jumped to 6♡, ending the auction.

West led the ♣J. South saw finessing chances in three side suits. He could win the ♣A, draw trump, and finesse spades to throw his club loser, a 50% play. He could finesse the ♣Q and if it lost, finesse the ◊Q later, a 75% line. He chose the 75% line.

Alas, both the ♣K and ◊K were offside. Two five-yard penalties but no loss of down---er, wrong sport, down one and a big loss of slam.

"Next time, try 'Eeny, meany, miney, moe,'" said North. Would that be an improvement?

Not really. But by now, you should see a 100% "second suit" line. Win the ♣A. Draw trump with the ♡AK and if necessary the ♡J. Cash the ♠A and lead the ♠Q. If covered, ruff; after returning to dummy to discard a club and two diamonds on spades, try a diamond finesse for an overtrick.

If not covered, discard your club. You may lose to the ♠K, but then dummy's remaining spades will provide three diamond pitches: 12 tricks guaranteed.

DEAL 132. A MIRAGE

```
              ♠ 8 3 2
              ♡ K 10 3
              ◊ 8 7 5 4 3
              ♣ A 3
  ♠ Q J 9 7              ♠ K 10 4
  ♡ 6 5 4                ♡ 2
  ◊ K 10                 ◊ J 9 6 2
  ♣ K 8 7 6              ♣ Q 10 9 4 2
              ♠ A 6 5
              ♡ A Q J 9 8 7
              ◊ A Q
              ♣ J 5
```

After a 1♡ – 2♡ – 4♡ auction, West led the ♠Q.

Declarer won the ♠A, cashed the ♡A, led to dummy's ♡10 and cashed dummy's ♡K when East showed out. Then he finessed the ◊Q.

West won the ◊K and continued spades. The defense scored two spade tricks and an eventual club trick. Down one.

"Tough luck," said North. "I can't blame you for bidding a fifty-percent game?"

Was she right?

Yes, but she could blame him for taking a 50% play when he had better. This deal is a mirage. If the ◊Q were the deuce, South might have found a higher-percentage line. Dummy has a five-card side suit, so first consider setting it up for a tenth trick.

Let's see how it works. At Trick 2, cash the ♡A, then lead the ◊A and surrender a diamond. The defenders can win, cash two spades and drive out dummy's ♣A.

But now a diamond ruff, a heart to dummy's ♡10, another diamond ruff and a heart to dummy's ♡K let South discard his last club on dummy's fifth diamond. An 84% line, and 10 easy tricks.

Timing is crucial. Declarer must not dally with a diamond finesse, he must stay a step ahead.

DEAL 133. BACK ME UP, PLEASE

```
              ♠ A
              ♡ 6 3 2
              ◊ A K 5 3 2
              ♣ A 9 6 3
♠ K J 9 8 5 2                    ♠ Q 10 7 6 3
♡ 9 4                           ♡ 8
◊ J 8 7 4                       ◊ Q 10 9 6
♣ J                             ♣ K Q 10
              ♠ 4
              ♡ A K Q J 10 7 5
              ◊ void
              ♣ 8 7 5 4 2
```

South opened 4♡ on adverse vulnerability and North bid 6♡.

Declarer won the spade opening lead in dummy and cashed the ♡AK. He ducked a club to West's ♣J. West shifted to the ◊4. Declarer discarded clubs on dummy's two top diamonds and cashed dummy's ♣A. When the clubs split 3-1, he lost another club trick. Down one.

Any better line?

Yes, a line that offers two ways to make: clubs 2-2 *or* diamonds 4-4. With one of dummy's entries gone, better start the diamonds at Trick 2. Ruff a diamond high, cash two high trumps.

Cross to dummy's ♣A, pitch two clubs on dummy's two top diamonds, and ruff another diamond high.

If diamonds split 4-4 as you now know they do, lead the low ♡5 to dummy's ♡6 and cash dummy's fifth diamond. That makes 12 tricks, but if diamonds do not split 4-4, you can still try your backup plan.

Lead a second club. A 2-2 club split will see you home just as well at the end of the dance as at the beginning.

DEAL 134. WHICH SUIT FIRST?

```
                    ♠ 3 2
                    ♡ A 8
                    ◊ Q 10 2
                    ♣ A Q 10 8 7 2
   ♠ A K 10 8 5                     ♠ Q 9 6 4
   ♡ 5 2                            ♡ J 10 9 4
   ◊ J 9 7 5                        ◊ 4
   ♣ 9 4                            ♣ K J 5 3
                    ♠ J 7
                    ♡ K Q 7 6 3
                    ◊ A K 8 6 3
                    ♣ 6
```

Despite favorable vulnerability and West's 1♠ overcall, after having jumped to 3♠ preemptively, East sold out to 4♡. Perhaps the soft bleating of the lambs should have warned South of the forthcoming bad splits.

West cashed both top spades and shifted to the ♣9. South won dummy's ♣A and drew three top trumps, West pitching the ♠8 on the third.
South led low to dummy's ◊Q and back to his ◊A as East threw a club. When South led the ◊K next, East ruffed with the master trump. South ruffed the next spade but was out of gas. West won the ◊J and a spade at the end. Down two.

Would you know how to keep your assets intact and bring home the bacon---er, your diamond side suit?

Let the defenders ruff air, not your high cards. After winning dummy's ♣A at Trick 3, arrange to lead low diamonds through East. ◊Q, then a low diamond.
East dare not ruff air with his trump trick. When he discards a club, win the ◊A, cross to dummy's ♡A and lead dummy's ◊10. Again, East dare not ruff air. Win the ◊K and ruff a diamond with dummy's low trump. Now East can ruff without blowing a trick but ... that's all for the defense.

If East still declines to ruff ...♣A, club ruff, ♡K, ♡Q and he can either ruff your fifth diamond with the master trump or wait with it to win Trick 13.
A second suit comes home again to let you make your game.

DEAL 135. ANNOYING

```
                        ♠ K J 9 7
                        ♡ void
                        ◊ A 10 7 5 2
                        ♣ J 6 5 3
        ♠ 6 3                           ♠ 4
        ♡ 10 7                          ♡ A Q J 9 8 5 2
        ◊ Q 9 6                         ◊ K 8 4 3
        ♣ K 10 9 8 4 2                  ♣ 7
                        ♠ A Q 10 8 5 2
                        ♡ K 6 4 3
                        ◊ J
                        ♣ A Q
```

When South overcalled East's 4♡ opening, North gambled 6♠.

Somehow West judged to lead the ♠3 instead of the ♡10. Did he guess that North's jump to 6♠ was based on an expectation of heart ruffs?

"Annoying," mumbled South so softly that even his kibitzer couldn't hear him. Without that trump lead he could have crossruffed for 12 tricks. After winning dummy's ♠7, South finessed the ♣Q, losing to West's ♣K.

"More annoying," he muttered audibly. And when West continued with the ♠6, South said "Enough! Now I'm really annoyed!" so loudly that Gertie ran out of the club's kitchen to offer aspirins to the table.

Now South unblocked his ♣A and turned his attention to diamonds. ◊A, heart discard on dummy's ♣J, diamond ruff. Heart ruff, a second diamond ruff, a second heart ruff, a third diamond ruff ... out of gas.

Dummy's ◊10 was now high, but he had no entry to reach it. Eventually, he lost the ♡K to East's ♡A. Down one.

Could you make 6♠ despite the annoying trump lead?

Yes. Don't give West a chance to lead another. At Trick 2, ◊A and ruff a diamond high. Ruff a heart, ruff another diamond. Cross to the ♠K, ruff a third diamond. ♣A, ♣Q to West's ♣K.

Now dummy's ◊10 and ♣J are good for two heart discards after you ruff another heart to reach them.

148

DEAL 136. WHICH SUIT IS THE SECOND SUIT?

```
                    ♠ 6 5
                    ♡ A K Q 4
                    ◊ A J 8 5 3
                    ♣ K 3
    ♠ K 8                             ♠ Q 7 4 2
    ♡ J 7                             ♡ 9 8 5 3
    ◊ K 9 6 3                         ◊ 10 2
    ♣ Q 10 9 6 2                      ♣ J 8 7
                    ♠ A J 10 9 3
                    ♡ 10 6 2
                    ◊ Q 7
                    ♣ A 5 4
```

South opened a slightly shaded 1♠, rebid 2♠ over North's 2◊ response, and bought the contract for 3NT after North rebid 3♡.

West led the ♣10, and South faced a problem immediately: in which of the three suits with a combined seven cards to develop tricks?

Realizing that his hand was short of entries after the defenders forced out his ♣A, he chose to make dummy the master hand and seek his tricks in the red suits.

After ducking the first club and winning the second in dummy, he led low towards his ◊Q, the best play in the suit as it catered no only to a 3-3 split but to East's possible ◊Kx. The ◊Q fell to West's ◊K and declarer threw a spade from dummy when a third club went to his ♣A.

When declarer cashed dummy's two diamond honors and three top hearts, West remained with the high ◊9 and East remained with the high ♡9. The ♠A was South's eighth and last trick. Down one.

Any way to come to a ninth after embarking on the same line?

Yes, by tending to the second suit, hearts. After winning the ♣A, declarer should cash dummy's royal heart couple. When the ♡J falls, he can lead to his ♡10 and only then cash dummy's ◊A and ◊J.

Two tricks in each minor, the ♠A, and *four* tricks in the second suit, hearts: total *nine*.

149

DEAL 137. DECLARE OR DEFEND?

```
                    ♠ A 7 6 5 2
                    ♡ 10 2
                    ◊ K 5 3
                    ♣ A 7 3
♠ Q J                                   ♠ K 10 9 3
♡ 7 6 4                                 ♡ 8 5
◊ J 10 9 8                              ◊ A Q 7 6
♣ Q 8 5 2                               ♣ 10 9 6
                    ♠ 8 4
                    ♡ A K Q J 9 3
                    ◊ 4 2
                    ♣ K J 4
```

South opened 1♡ and North bid 1♠. South rebid 2♡, which shows six because it bypasses four other bids, so North invited game with 3♡ and South bid 4♡.

West led the ◊J and continued with the ◊10 when it held, as East encouraged with the ◊7 and then the ◊6.

South ruffed the third diamond, drew trump, and relied on a club finesse for his tenth trick. It lost; down one.

Was this the best plan? How would you have declared 4♡?

Playing on spades, an 84% line, is better. Duck a spade at Trick 4. Dummy's ♠A, ♡10 and ♣A are the three entries you need to set up and cash dummy's fifth spade for a club discard and avoid a club finesse.

Note that better defense can thwart this plan. If West leads the ◊8, *bottom of his sequence*, to Trick 2, East can figure out to win the ◊Q and shift to the ♣10, attacking dummy's ♣A entry.

South can parry by rising with the ♣K, but then East can counter by overtaking West's ♠J to continue clubs when declarer ducks a spade. Thrust and counterthrust!

Oh yes. Had North rebid 2NT at his second turn, South would have bid the cold 3NT. 3NT might be best even from South's side, as only diamond lead and a 5-3 diamond split with the ◊A offside can beat it.

CHAPTER 9
Defense

DEAL 138. WAIT, I'M NOT READY TO USE IT

                         ♠ Q J 3
                         ♡ Q 8
                         ◊ Q 4
                         ♣ A Q J 8 7 3
        ♠ K 8 4   ♠ 9 6 5 2
        ♡ K 4 2   ♡ 7 5
        ◊ A K 8 7   ◊ J 10 9 5 3
        ♣ 10 5 2   ♣ 9 4
                         A 10 7
                         ♡ A J 10 9 6 3
                         ◊ 6 2
                         ♣ K 6

♠North-South reached 4♡ after South opened 1♡ and rebid 2♡ over North's 2♣ response, which they played as game-forcing.

Using Patriarch Opening Leads, in which the lead of a king normally promises the queen, West led the ◊A. East played the ◊J, showing the ◊10, so West cashed the ◊K and shifted to the ♡2.

Declarer put up dummy's ♡Q and finessed the ♡J when it held.

Dummy's trumps being gone, West continued with a third diamond, expecting East to win the ◊10, but declarer ruffed, drew the last trump and ran clubs to take the rest.

Could 4♡ have been beaten?

Yes. On the auction East could hardly have any assets besides the ◊J10. So West needed to attack the only entries dummy could have that would be useful later,

As dummy's entries were in the club suit itself, that, not a trump, was the suit to attack. Then, upon winning the ♡K, West could lead another club to *kill the dummy* and wait for the setting trick in spades.

DEAL 139. NO THANKS

                    ♠ 4 3
                    ♡ K Q 10 9 8 3
                    ◊ K J 8 4
                    ♣ J

♠ Q 8 6 5   ♠ 7
♡ void   ♡ 7 6 5 4 2
◊ A Q 10 9 7 2   ◊ 6 5 3
♣ K Q 10   ♣ 9 7 6 2

                    ♠ A K J 10 9 2
                    ♡ A J
                    ◊ void
                    ♣ A 8 5 4 3

South opened 1♠ and West overcalled 2◊. North bid 2♡ and South jumped to 3♠. When North raised to 4♠, South gambled 6♠.

West led the ♣K to declarer's ♣A To keep control and a trump in dummy led the ♠J. West won the ♠Q. Declarer had the rest.

Could you beat this slam?

When a good declarer offers you a gift, it's best to think twice before taking it. Why is he being so good to you? Has he played the wrong card? Highly unlikely. If West ducks the ♠Q, declarer is finished.

If declarer continues trumps, West will get in and take club tricks. A crafty declarer can lead the ♡A, but West can again refrain from winning his trump trick prematurely and ruff the ♡J after East has given count to show an odd number of hearts.

Could South have done better?

Yes, if he hadn't been so eager to declare and so certain that the contract belonged in spades. Had he rebid 3♣, they might have reached 6♡. Contracts often play better in the suit of the partner with the weaker hand. Do you think that East could find the club lead needed to beat 6♡?

DEAL 140. REMOVING THE ENTRY

<pre>
                      ♠ 6 3 2
                      ♡ A J 10 5 4
                      ◊ 5 2
                      ♣ K J 4
      ♠ J 9 8 4   ♠ Q 10 5
      ♡ K 7 6   ♡ Q 9 3 2
      ◊ A 10 8 3   ◊ K J 9 6 4
      ♣ 6 3   ♣ 7
                      ♠ A K 7
                      ♡ 8
                      ◊ Q 7
                      ♣ A Q 10 9 8 5 2
</pre>

South opened 1♣ and jumped to 3♣ over North 1♡ response. When North rebid his nice five-card heart suit, South angled for 3NT by bidding 3♠ to show he had spades well stopped. Unable to supply a diamond stopper, North gambled 5♣.

Guided by the auction, West led the ◊A. East encouraged with the ◊9, so West continued with the ◊3 to East's ◊K. East shifted to the ♠5 "through declarer's strength" as he said during the post-mortem.

South won the ♠A and got to work ruffing out dummy's five-card heart suit. Taking care to preserve the ♣2 to lead to dummy's ♣4 later, he was able to establish and use dummy's fifth heart. Making 5♣.

Were the defenders helpless to stop declarer?

Not exactly. The key to defending when dummy has a long suit is to attack dummy's outside entries. Here those entries were trumps. A trump shift at Trick 3 scuttles the contract.

Jim and Danny disagree about this deal. Jim approves South's bidding. Danny doesn't. "Why not gamble three notrump over North's three hearts?" he says. "Ten fast tricks. They always lead the unbid major against three notrump, don't they? Look at the West hand: wouldn't you lead a spade?"

DEAL 141. DECLARE OR DEFEND?

```
                        ♠ 4
                        ♡ A K 10 7 5 3
                        ◇ Q 9 2
                        ♣ K 7 6
     ♠ 10 8 5                              ♠ A K J 9 7 3
     ♡ Q 6 2                               ♡ J 9 4
     ◇ K 7 5 3                             ◇ J 10 8
     ♣ 9 8 4                               ♣ 5
                        ♠ Q 6 2
                        ♡ 8
                        ◇ A 6 4
                        ♣ A Q J 10 3 2
```

East's Weak 2♠ Bid as dealer with both sides vulnerable had the perverse effect of pushing his opponents into a 6♣ slam when South overcalled 3♣. Left to themselves, North and South might have stopped in game.

West led the ♠5 to East's ♠K. East shifted promptly to the ◇J, hoping that West had the ◇K.

Thinking East extremely unlikely to have the ◇K, South rose with the ◇A, Placing West with the ◇K on the auction, and thus needing to dump two diamonds, South took his only realistic chance, ruffing out the hearts.

◇A, ♡K, ♡A, heart ruffed high. ♣Q, ♣J and over to dummy's ♣K to run the hearts that fortunately split 3-3. One diamond, five hearts, and six clubs gave declarer the 12 tricks he needed for slam.

Could the defenders have beaten 6♣?

Yes. What's the best defense against a second suit? Kill the dummy! Attack dummy's entries. Chessplayers are familiar with spectacular queen sacrifices. Here East had a chance to make a play that chessplayers might envy: an ace sacrifice. Lead the ♠A to Trick 2, forcing dummy to ruff.

Declarer can set up the hearts, but won't be able to cash the ones he sets up ... for lack of a dummy entry.

DEAL 142. TWO SUITS

        ♠ A Q 6 3
        ♡ K Q 6 2
        ◊ Q 6 5 3
        ♣ 6

♠ J 10 8 2   ♠ K 9 7 4
♡ J 10 9 4   ♡ A 8 7
◊ 8   ◊ 9 7 4 2
♣ Q 10 9 3   ♣ 5 4

        ♠ 5
        ♡ 5 3
        ◊ A K J 10
        ♣ A K J 8 7 2

South opened 1♣ and "reversed" into 2◊, forcing, promising a strong hand with longer clubs than diamonds and a third bid. North's 3◊ raise promised four-card support and game values, as only a two-level rebid might be minimum.

South's 4♣ next showed a sixth club, and when North cue-bid 4♠, South bid 6◊ on the strength of his "chunky" diamonds.

South covered West's ♡J opening lead with dummy's ♡Q. East won the ♡A and returned the ♡8 to dummy's ♡K.

Now declarer set up his clubs. ♣A, ruff a club, back to his hand with a trump, ruff a club with dummy's ◊Q, back to his hand with dummy's last trump and draw the rest of the trumps. ♣K, more clubs, and claim 12 tricks.

Could the defense have prevailed?

Yes. East can beat 6◊ with a trump shift at Trick 2, driving out one of declarer's entries before he can use it to ruff out the clubs.

West can beat 6◊ by leading the ♠J to drive out dummy's ♠A before declarer can set up a heart trick for a twelfth winner. (If declarer leads hearts himself, East can win the ♡A and lead the ♠K to shorten his trumps.) An opening trump lead, which is often effective in "second suit" deals, also wrecks declarer's transportation.

DEAL 143. CAREFUL

North
♠ A J
♡ A Q J 3
◊ K Q J 10 4
♣ K 5

East
♠ K 9 5
♡ 8 4 2
◊ A 3
♣ A Q 9 4 3

West responded 1♠ to East's 1♣ opening. Unaccountably, East failed to raise to 2♠, letting South bid hearts at the two-level. North raised to 4♡.

West led the ♣10 against 4♡. East won the ♣Q. Besides his two aces, East saw no hope for another trick except in spades. As a spade trick might disappear on dummy's diamonds once declarer drives out the ◊A, East cashed the ♣A and shifted to the ♠5.

Was this the right defense?

Not quite. Yes, the defense needs a quick spade trick. But what the defense doesn't need is to take the ♣A before the spade trick can be set up. West's ♣10 opening lead denies the ♣J, so cashing the ♣A makes South's ♣J high, allowing declarer to discard dummy's ♠J.

Might West have ♠Q10732 ♡K ◊87652 ♣107 or even as little as ♠Q10732 ♡9 ◊87652 ♣107? Yes. So East must shift to spades *forthwith*.

Another case of "Cash an Ace, Blow a Trick!": a mantra that Danny claims to have received in his youth, when pilgrimages to the Himalayas were fashionable, from the Maharishi Mahesh Daniel himself. In his old age, Danny came to believe otherwise.

We're sorry to shake your faith in Maharishis, but cashing an ace blows one trick only on a good day. On a bad day, it blows several.

DEAL 144. NOTHING TO LOSE

```
                    ♠ A J
                    ♡ J 10 3
                    ◇ K Q J 10 7
                    ♣ J 10 3
    ♠ K 5 3                        ♠ Q 10 9 7 4 2
    ♡ 8 5 2                        ♡ 6
    ◇ A 8 3                        ◇ 9 4
    ♣ A K 7 2                      ♣ 9 8 6 4
                    ♠ 8 6
                    ♡ A K Q 9 7 4
                    ◇ 6 5 2
                    ♣ Q 5
```

Vulnerable against not, West wisely refrained from entering the auction after South responded 1♡ to North's 1◇ opening. North and South marched merrily to 4♡: North rebid 1NT and South invited with 3♡. North accepted with three-card support, a side suit as a source of tricks, and an outside ace.

Using Patriarch Opening Leads, West led the ♣A, normally showing the ♣K. East played a discouraging ♣4. West knew from the auction that East was almost broke. But might he be able to give East a diamond ruff?

He cashed the ◇A and led a second diamond. Declarer scored six heart tricks, four diamond tricks, and one spade, 11 tricks in all.

It's a "second suit" deal. Any better ideas for West?

Yes, East is "almost" broke. But there is room in his hand for a queen. It sure isn't a minor-suit queen and if it's the ♡Q it's about to fall singleton. How about switching to a spade in hope East has the ♠Q? Is that dangerous?

No. After dislodging the ◇A, will find plenty of tricks available without scoring a second spade trick. It's now or never for a spade shift, before dummy's diamonds are ready to roll. When East does have the ♠Q, the defenders will take four tricks to beat 4♡.

DEAL 145. ME TOO, NOTHING TO LOSE

```
                    ♠ J 7 5
                    ♡ Q
                    ◇ K 8 6 4
                    ♣ K J 10 9 7
    ♠ Q 6 4 3                      ♠ K 2
    ♡ J 10 6 3                     ♡ A K 8 4 2
    ◇ 9 7                          ◇ 10 3
    ♣ 6 3 2                        ♣ A Q 5 4
                    ♠ A 10 9 8
                    ♡ 9 7 5
                    ◇ A Q J 5 2
                    ♣ 8
```

With nobody vul, both pairs engaged in a free-for-all. South opened 1◇ and made a slightly shaded limit raise. That didn't silence East, who had opening-bid strength plus extras and bid 3♡. South who might have had a balanced 13 HCP and four mediocre diamonds for his opening, liked his shape and strong five-bagger well enough to compete to 4◇ and West bid 4♡ in an attempt to push his opponents overboard. He succeeded, East doubled 5◇ and started salivating.

West led the ♡J. East, with the ♣AQ well placed behind dummy, chose to stay passive. After winning the ♡K he returned the ♡4. Declarer ruffed West's ♡10 in dummy, led to his ◇Q and finessed dummy's ♣J. East won the ♣Q and tapped dummy again with the ♡A.

Now he led dummy's ♣K, ruffed off East's ♣A, and crossed to dummy's ◇K. When both defenders followed, he dumped three spades on dummy's clubs to make 5◇ doubled.

Could the defenders have beaten the contract?

Yes. If South had both the ♠A and the ♠Q, East's ♠K was toast. So he might as well lead it to Trick 2 while he still had dummy's clubs stopped. Everything to gain and nothing to lose.

South would need to take care to draw East's trumps before leading either black suit, else the ♠Q and a spade ruff would beat 5◇ doubled *two*.

DEAL 146. AN UNUSUAL OVERTAKE

```
                        ♠ void
                        ♡ J
                        ◊ K 7 6 5 4 2
                        ♣ A K J 9 8 6
♠ J 10 7 5                                   ♠ A Q
♡ A 10 6 3                                   ♡ K 9 7 5 4 2
◊ Q 10 9 8                                   ◊ A 3
♣ 3                                          ♣ 5 4 2
                        ♠ K 9 8 6 4 3 2
                        ♡ Q 8
                        ◊ J
                        ♣ Q 10 7
```

East opened 1♡. South made a weak jump overcall and West had an easy 3♡ raise. North bid 4NT for the minors. South's 5♣ ended the auction.

"No aces?" asked West before leading.

"Yes, we don't play '1430' or any other fancy kind of Blackwood," answered South with a wink. Then "Kidding---I prefer clubs to diamonds."

West led the ♡A and shifted safely to the ♣2. South won the ♣Q. Ruffing out the spades looked impossible, but could he set up diamonds? South led the ◊J. West covered with the ◊Q.

Reading East for the ◊A, declarer let West's ◊Q hold. West tapped dummy with a heart. East's ◊A fell on the next diamond. South ruffed and was able to ruff another diamond with his last trump. Soon dummy was high.

Could 5♣ have been beaten?

Yes! Had East overtaken West's ◊Q with his doomed ◊A and led another trump, South could not ruff the suit out and would eventually lose another diamond. Should we blame East for failing to do so?

No. We think East blameless. For all he could tell, South may have had ◊J9 or ◊J8 *doubleton*. In that case, overtaking would be fatal. We blame *West*, who could tell what was going on. By playing the ◊10 (a most revealing card!) under South's ◊J, he could *induce* East to go right.

DEAL 147. TAKE OVER

♠ J 9 8 6
♡ J 7 3
◊ A 7
♣ J 10 9 8

♠ A
♡ K Q 10 5 4
◊ K 8 5 2
♣ K 3 2

♠ 4
♡ A 9 8 2
◊ J 10 9 4 3
♣ 7 6 4

♠ K Q 10 7 5 3 2
♡ 6
◊ Q 6
♣ A Q 5

West opened 1♡ and East raised to 2♡. South bid 2♠ and North took what he thought was a 4♠ "save" over West's 4♡. West led the ♡K.

East encouraged with the ♡9 and West continued with the ♡5. South ruffed and led the ♠Q to West's ♠A. Not wanting to lead from either of his minor-suit kings, West exited with the ♡Q.

South ruffed and crossed to dummy with a trump to take a club finesse.

West won, but that was the last trick for the defense. Declarer's diamond loser went away on the long clubs.

Here we go again. Who's to blame this time?

This time it's East. He knows the defense has only one heart trick coming. Forget signaling! Overtake the ♡K with the ♡A at Trick 1 and shift to the ◊J before those long clubs are set up.

Declarer loses one trick in each suit, down one.

DEAL 148. SORRY, IT LOOKED SO SAFE

```
                          ♠ K 4 2
                          ♡ 10 8 5
                          ♢ A Q
                          ♣ 7 5 4 3 2
        ♠ 5                               ♠ A
        ♡ J 7 4 2                         ♡ Q 9 6
        ♢ 9 6 5 2                         ♢ J 10 7 4 3
        ♣ A Q 9 6                         ♣ K J 10 8
                          ♠ Q J 10 9 8 7 6 3
                          ♡ A K 3
                          ♢ K 8
                          ♣ void
```

South opened 1♠. The last thing he expected was silence from the opponents and a simple 2♠ raise from North, but that's what he got. Slam was suddenly on the horizon. He jumped to 4♣, an "autosplinter" showing club shortness and slam hopes. Having nothing wasted in clubs, North cooperated with a 4♢ cue bid showing the ♢A.

Might North have ace-fourth in both spades and diamonds? Nah, too much to hope! South muttered "No greed," as he settled for 6♠.

East won West's trump lead with the ♠A as South followed with the ♠6. What now? A diamond shift up to dummy's ♢AQ. No Thanks! Hearts? Not declarer's likely side suit! But if South's 4♣ autosplinter were based on a low singleton ...? He shifted to the ♣J.

That saved South one dummy entry. He ruffed high. Two diamond entries and the ♠K let him ruff three more clubs high. When clubs split 4-4, he led his carefully-preserved ♠3 to dummy and threw his ♡3 on the ♣7.

Could the defenders have seen it coming?

Yes, this was a "second suit" deal. As usual, "Kill the dummy!" applied. A low heart would also work, but a diamond shift is thematic.

"The club looked so safe," muttered East as he scored up 1430 for the opponents and rose from his chair to change for the next rubber.

DEAL 149. WIN OR DUCK?

♠ K Q 8 4 2
♡ Q 10 3
♢ 10 6
♣ 8 6 4

♠ 9 5
♡ 7 6 2
♢ K Q 9 3
♣ K 9 7 2

♠ A J 10 6
♡ 5
♢ J 7 5 4 2
♣ Q J 10

♠ 7 3
♡ A K J 9 8 4
♢ A 8
♣ A 5 3

South reached 4♡ via a 1♡ – 2♡ – 4♡ auction. West led the ♢K.

Declarer won the ♢A and led the ♠3 to West's ♠9 and dummy's ♠K. East won the ♠A, cashed the ♢J and switched to the ♣Q.

South won the ♣A, led to the ♠Q, and ruffed a spade high. He led to the ♡10, and ruffed another spade high, setting up dummy's fifth spade.

The ♡J and a third heart to dummy's ♡Q drew the last trumps, and dummy's ♠8 provided a tenth trick.

Was this a "routine make" or could the defenders have beaten 4♡?

West defended well to have played the ♠9 on the first spade, showing count. That told East he didn't have three spades. Therefore East can duck the first spade safely,

Declarer always has three entries to dummy, but the spade entry is useful only when declarer is ready to ruff a spade. By letting dummy win a spade trick when the entry does declarer no good, East will beat 4♡.

DEAL 150. REMOVING AN ENTRY

```
                          ♠ 2
                          ♡ A K 10 7 5 3
                          ◊ K 9 4
                          ♣ Q 8 3
        ♠ 10 8 7 6                        ♠ A K 9 5 3
        ♡ J 8 2                           ♡ Q 9 6
        ◊ 7 6 5                           ◊ 8
        ♣ K 6 4                           ♣ J 10 9 2
                          ♠ Q J 4
                          ♡ 4
                          ◊ A Q J 10 3 2
                          ♣ A 7 5
```

North opened 1♡ and South responded 2◊, which they played as forcing to game even over East's 1♠ overcall. With less than game values, an invitational 3◊ jump was available to South.

South rebid 2NT, figuring that he'd better show that he had spades stopped before things got out of hand. This nice "slow" 2/1 GF auction let North bid 3◊ without fear of being passed. South visualized North's 1=6=3=3 pattern and cue-bid 4♣. That spurred North to gamble 6◊.

West led the ♠6 against 6◊. East won the ♠K and shifted to the ♣J. Declarer saw that ruffing two spades would only bring eleven tricks. He won the ♣A. He took two top hearts ruffed a heart high. Lucky, 3-3 hearts. But even 4-2 hearts would have brought the slam home if trumps were 2-2.

Could the defenders have beaten 6◊?

Yes, had East remembered the best defense when dummy has a long side suit: *Kill the dummy!* So, instead of a passive club shift, lead that ♠A to Trick 2.
Declarer must ruff in dummy. Now the crucial *third-round* trump entry to dummy disappears, and along with it, all hope to make 6◊ when trumps split 3-1.

DEAL 151. HELP PARTNER OUT

♠ Q 9 2
♡ A J 7
◊ Q 2
♣ J 9 8 7 2

♠ 8   ♠ A K J 10 5 4
♡ 6 5 4   ♡ 3
◊ K 9 8 7 6   ◊ J 10 4 3
♣ Q 10 5 3   ♣ 6 4

♠ 7 6 3
♡ K Q 10 9 8 2
◊ A 5
♣ A K

South opened 1♡ and North raised to 2♡. East bid 2♠ and South bid 4♡. West led the ♠8.

East won the first three spade tricks, West discarding diamonds. East switched to the ◊J. South won and cashed the ♣AK. He led a trump to dummy's ♡7, ruffed a club, crossed to the ♡J and ruffed another club.

Declarer then crossed to dummy's ♡A, drawing West's last trump, and discarded his low diamond on the good fifth club. Making 4♡.

Whose fault this time?

Not East's. Yes, East could have beaten 4♡ with a killing trump shift at Trick 4, but East was in no position to know what was going on. Might South have had ◊AK and ♣AQ? Or ◊AK and ♣AK but a fragile ♡Q98652?

Only West could see the club threat and know to remove a trump entry from dummy. So West could ruff the third spade and lead a trump himself.

DEAL 152. WHAT'S THE HURRY?

```
                      ♠ 10 9
                      ♡ K J 9 2
                      ◊ K J 8 4 3
                      ♣ K 4
        ♠ K 8 6 4 2                      ♠ J 7 5 3
        ♡ 8 5                            ♡ A 7 3
        ◊ 9                              ◊ A 6 5 2
        ♣ Q 10 7 6 2                     ♣ J 9
                      ♠ A Q
                      ♡ Q 10 6 4
                      ◊ Q 10 7
                      ♣ A 8 5 3
```

South opened 1♣ and rebid 1♡ over North's 1◊ response, then accepted North's 3♡ game invitation.

West led the ◊9. South dropped the ◊10 under East's ◊A, but East said, "Do you think I was born yesterday? You can't fool me!"

"Sorry I even tried," apologized South when East's ◊2 return hit the table. "I won't do it again."

True to her word, South followed with the ◊7. West ruffed and shifted to the ♣J. South won in hand and led low to dummy's ♡J. East took the ♡A and led a third diamond. South won the ◊Q and drew trump in two more rounds. She threw a club and the ♠Q on dummy's ◊KJ and claimed the rest.

"Who asked you to give me a ruff?" said West sarcastically.

Can we forgive her sarcasm?

Yes. East could tell from the auction that there was no hurry to give West a ruff. That could wait until he got in with the ♡A on the first trump lead. But if West had the ♠K, East had to shift to spades promptly. West probably couldn't lead spades without blowing a trick.

Giving the ruff prematurely left West without an effective return.

DEAL 153. DANNY'S BIRTHDAY

The Kantar 3NT opening shows a running seven-card major with about 7-7½ playing tricks. The Kleinman 3NT is similar but shows an ace more, nearly enough for an artificial forcing 2♣. That's what South opened. North's 4◊ response asked for the major; South's 4♡ ended the auction.

                    ♠ Q 10 8
                    ♡ 7 3
                    ◊ K Q 9 5
                    ♣ 7 6 4 3
    ♠ K 7 4
    ♡ 8 5
    ◊ A 10 7 4
    ♣ A K 10 8

Using old-fashioned leads, you start with the ♣K and catch the ♣9 from East and the ♣5 from declarer. You continue with the ♣A which drops South's ♣J as partner plays the ♣2. South ruffs the next club and cashes the ♡AK as partner's ♡J falls, Here comes declarer's ◊J: Win or Duck?

Too late now! South has ♠AJ ♡AKQ10964 ◊J3 ♣J5. If you win the ◊A, he'll dump the ♠J on dummy's ◊KQ. If you duck, he'll squeeze-endplay you, running trumps and sticking you in with the ◊A at Trick 11 to lead from ♠Kx.

You had to lead low to partner's ♣Q at Trick 2 to get a spade back. That's the winning play when partner has ♣Q92. Your play works when he has ♣92. (The play to Trick 1 marks South with the ♣J.) A guess?

Not quite. In the layouts where your play makes a difference, the choice boils down to one card: the ♣Q. Who has it?

What are the odds that South has the ♣Q? They're *not* even money. Given that South has ♣J5, the ♠A, and at least 7 hearts, there are 3 "open spaces" into which the ♣Q can fit. Given that East has ♣92 and at least 1 heart, there are 10 "open spaces" into which the ♣Q can fit.

Therefore. the chances that South has the ♣Q are 3/(10+3) = 3/13. That's Danny's Birthday. South is much less likely than East to have the ♣Q. So lead the ♣8 to East's ♣Q. Today is your lucky day: it works.

DEAL 154. TIMING

```
                        ♠ 6 4 3
                        ♡ 9 8 7
                        ◊ J 5
                        ♣ A Q 10 7 2
    ♠ Q J 10 9                        ♠ 8
    ♡ J 10 6 2                        ♡ Q 5
    ◊ Q 8 3                           ◊ A K 10 9 7 6 4
    ♣ 9 6                             ♣ J 8 5
                        ♠ A K 7 5 2
                        ♡ A K 4 3
                        ◊ 2
                        ♣ K 4 3
```

South opened 1♠ and North replied 1NT, which they played as forcing. East took advantage of favorable vulnerability to preempt 4◊. Undeterred, South bid 4♡ with his fine hand. West doubled, and doubled again when North's 4♠ preference came round to him.

West led the ◊3 to East's ◊K. South ruffed East's ◊A continuation and ducked a spade. Unwilling to give offer a ruff-sluff with his last diamond, West shifted to the ♡2.

The race was on. South captured East's ♡Q with the ♡A and ducked another trump to West, but now declarer was in control. He won the ♡K, finished trumps, and ran clubs to take the rest. Making 4♠ doubled.

"Why did you double?" screamed East "I didn't promise any defense."

"Down one if you knew how to defend," countered West.

Who was to blame? *Dr J's Law* says, "Usually the partner who yells first." How would you have defended?

Diamond taps didn't figure to succeed, for declarer could ruff diamonds in dummy. This was a race, as "second suit" deals often are. Here the defenders needed to set up a heart trick before declarer could take control. A heart shift from East at Trick 2 puts the defense one step ahead and wins the race. West gets a heart trick in time. Down one.

DEAL 155. ACTIVE OR PASSIVE?

```
                    ♠ A Q 6 5 2
                    ♡ 8 7
                    ◊ Q 10 7
                    ♣ 8 5 4
   ♠ 10 7 4 3                        ♠ J 9
   ♡ A J 10 3 2                      ♡ K Q 9 5
   ◊ 9 8 2                           ◊ A K J 4 3
   ♣ 7                               ♣ 3 2
                    ♠ K 8
                    ♡ 6 4
                    ◊ 6 5
                    ♣ A K Q J 10 9 6
```

East opened 1◊ and West made a "Negative Double" after South overcalled 2♣.
North bid 2♠ and East bid a pushy 3♡. Push came to shove when South pushed to 4♣,
West pushed to 4♡ and North pushed to 5♣. Not knowing who was saving against
whom, the players shoved their bidding cards into their bidding boxes.

Never having raised diamonds, West led the ◊2, showing length instead of denying
strength with a normal ◊9 lead.

East won the ◊J, ◊K and ◊A ... oops, the ◊A didn't win. South said, "Ace on ace,"
ruffing with the ♣A, and drew trump with the ♣KQ. The ♠K, ♠Q and ♠A let declarer
dump one heart.

He ruffed a fourth spade high, led the ♣6 to dummy's ♣8, and dumped his last
heart on dummy's fifth spade. He made 5♣ even though the defenders could have won
the first four tricks.

Which defender bears the blame?

East. He could tell no more than two diamond tricks were available, so at either
Trick 2 or Trick 3 he should have shifted to the ♡K ... before declarer could obtain the
lead and discard on dummy's spades.

DEAL 156. ANOTHER "SHORT" SECOND SUIT

```
                    ♠ 9 6 4
                    ♡ Q 6 2
                    ◊ K 10 3
                    ♣ 10 4 3 2
    ♠ 2                              ♠ J 8 7
    ♡ K 10 9 8 4                     ♡ A J 7
    ◊ Q 6 5 2                        ◊ J 9 7
    ♣ A Q 9                          ♣ 8 7 6 5
                    ♠ A K Q 10 5 3
                    ♡ 5 3
                    ◊ A 8 4
                    ♣ K J
```

West opened 1♡; East raised to 2♡. Fearing to miss a game, South jumped to 3♠. If you think this is a *weak* jump, go back to your barn and lock the door lest the cattle rustlers return to see if they left a calf behind.

West led the ♡10 against 3♡, and continued with the ♡8 when it held.
East won the ♡J and tried to cash the ♡A, but declarer ruffed. He drew trump and crossed to dummy's ◊K to finesse against East's hoped-for ♣Q.

No luck. West won the ♣Q and exited in diamonds. East's ◊9 drove out declarer's ◊A. West won the next club and cashed the ◊Q to beat 3♠.

Who erred this time?

Declarer erred. Instead of trying to avoid losing to East's possible ♣Q, he should have made sure of winning a trick with dummy's ♣10. After drawing trump, South should lead either the ♣K or the ♣J from his hand, losing two clubs quickly in time to set up the ♣10 before the defenders can drive out both top diamonds to set up a diamond trick for themselves.

Oh yes, East slipped too. The best defense on a "second suit" deal is normally to attack dummy's entries. Upon winning the ♡J at Trick 2, East should shift to the ◊7, attacking dummy's ◊K.
Now the defense is a step ahead, establishing the setting trick in diamonds before declarer can establish the fulfilling trick in clubs. Down one.

DEAL 157. WHAT TO LEAD?

$$\spadesuit Q\,5\,2$$
$$\heartsuit Q\,8\,7\,6\,2$$
$$\diamond 5$$
$$\clubsuit A\,K\,5\,3$$

♠ 9 8 4   ♠ 7
♡ K J 9   ♡ A 10 4 3
◊ Q 7 6   ◊ A K 10 8 3 2
♣ Q 9 7 2   ♣ J 8

$$\spadesuit A\,K\,J\,10\,6\,3$$
$$\heartsuit 5$$
$$\diamond J\,9\,4$$
$$\clubsuit 10\,6\,4$$

With both sides vul, East opened 1◊ and South jumped to 2♠, which he and his partner played as weak. West was unable to act, but North, being assured of a good six-card suit opposite, was able to bid 4♠.

West led the ◊6. East won the ◊K. Eager to prevent diamond ruffs in dummy, he shifted to the ♠7. South won the ♠A and led the ♡5. West hopped up with the ♡K to continue trumps.

South took dummy's ♠Q, ruffed a heart, ruffed a diamond with dummy's last trump, ruffed a second heart and drew the last trump, discarding the ♣3 from dummy. A club to dummy's ♣K, a third heart ruff with declarer's last trump, and another club put dummy in to cash the long ♡Q. That was declarer's tenth trick. 4♠ made.

Could the defenders have beaten 4♠? If so, with what defensive plan? And how could they know dummy's to embark on that plan?

West had 8 of the 40 "4-3-2-1" points in the deck, 6 of them in the unbid suits, and his partner had opened the bidding. On what could North and South be relying when they blasted into game?

Shape, including ruffs. So West start trumps, without delay. He'll get in twice more, with his ♡K and ◊Q, to draw more trumps. Declarer won't have time enough both to ruff out hearts and ruff a diamond in dummy. Nine tricks will be the limit, and down he'll go in 4♠.

DEAL 158. WHAT'S YOUR LEAD?

You, West, hold ♠K3 ♡8642 ◊Q10975 ♣J10. South deals and bids 2♣, his partnership's artificial powerhouse opening. North "waits" with a neutral 2◊ response, sensibly staying out of South's way, but bids a natural positive 2♠ over South's 2♡ rebid.

Notice how badly the auction could go if North were permitted to bid a natural positive 2♠ directly over 2♣. The only natural positive response that does more good than harm is 2♡, as South is unlikely to want to rebid 2♡ himself, but when he does, the sky's the limit.

South's 3♡ next shows a sixth heart, and North's 4♡ raise agrees on hearts. South uses Roman Keycard Blackwood to ask for keys in hearts North's replies show one key and the ◊K. South's 6♡ ends the auction.

What should you lead?

If you've been following our discussion of "second suit" deals, you'll know to *attack dummy's entries*. The ◊K is surely a dummy entry, perhaps even the only outside entry, to the spades. So lead the ◊5.

The whole deal:

```
                    ♠ A 8 7 5 4 2
                    ♡ 8 4
                    ◊ K 2
                    ♣ 8 6 2
        ♠ K 3                        ♠ Q 10 6
        ♡ 9 8 6 2                    ♡ 3
        ◊ Q 8 7 5                    ◊ J 10 6 4 3
        ♣ J 10 9                     ♣ Q 5 4 3
                    ♠ J 9
                    ♡ A K Q J 10 5
                    ◊ A 9
                    ♣ A K 7
```

Do you see it? After winning a spade trick, the defenders can continue diamonds to remove dummy's ◊K entry. But if you don't lead diamonds, declarer can duck a spade to set up the suit with a ruff while dummy's ◊K is still available to reach dummy.

DEAL 159. BEAT THAT!

$$\spadesuit \text{K J 10 4}$$
$$\heartsuit \text{10 5 2}$$
$$\diamondsuit \text{5}$$
$$\clubsuit \text{A J 10 9 7}$$

♠ 9 5 2	♠ A Q 7 6
♡ A Q 9	♡ 3
◊ 9 7 6 3	◊ A J 10 8 2
♣ K 5 3	♣ Q 4 2

$$\spadesuit \text{8 3}$$
$$\heartsuit \text{K J 8 7 6 4}$$
$$\diamondsuit \text{K Q 4}$$
$$\clubsuit \text{8 6}$$

East opened 1◊ and South overcalled 1♡. West bid 1NT and North's 2♡ raise ended the auction. West led the ◊3.

East won the ◊A and shifted to the ♡3, trying to eliminate dummy's ruffing entries. He succeeded; West cleared trumps. After winning the third trump, declarer led the ♠3 and finessed dummy's ♠10.

Dummy's trumps having been extracted, East returned the ◊J, hoping either to drive out South's ◊K, or pickle South's ◊Q if West had the ◊K. Curtains! South won the ◊K and drove out East's ♠A. Declarer wound up with four heart tricks, two diamonds, and one trick each in the black suits. Making 2♡.

Could East and West have done better?

Yes. After winning the ♠Q, East could have found a spectacular shift, leading the ♣2 into the belly of the whale. Declarer had chosen dummy's shorter suit as the "second suit" to establish an eighth trick, as dummy's longer club suit was the one with the sure entry. So, attack clubs!

West could have done better also. Leading a "second highest from length and weakness" ◊7 instead of a "fourth highest" ◊3 would have clarified the deal for East.

But do you see what else West could have done better? Think about it: what would happen had West raised to 2◊ at his first turn and ventured 2NT at his second? East would return to 3◊: beat that!

DEAL 160. NO OUTSIDE ENTRY?

```
                        ♠ J
                        ♡ 6 4 2
                        ◊ J 10 6
                        ♣ A K Q J 7 4
    ♠ Q 9 6 5                              ♠ 3 2
    ♡ Q 10 7 5                             ♡ 8 3
    ◊ A K 9                                ◊ Q 7 5 4 3 2
    ♣ 10 2                                 ♣ 9 8 6
                        ♠ A K 10 8 7 4
                        ♡ A K J 9
                        ◊ 8
                        ♣ 5 3
```

South opened 1♠ and rebid 2♡ over North's standard 2♣ response. North bid 3♣, delivering his promised rebid, but now South's 3♠ showed six spades and was forcing. North's 4♠ raise ended the auction.

Playing "A from AKx ..." opening leads, West led the ◊A. East played the ◊7 to encourage, so West continued with the ◊K. Declarer ruffed and led the ♠7 to dummy's ♠J. When it held, he came to the ♡A, cashed the ♠AK and surrendered a spade to West. That was the last trick for the defense. 4♠ made with an overtrick.

Could the defenders have found a way to beat 4♠?

Yes, if *both* defenders had appreciated the danger of dummy's running clubs and the need to kill dummy's entry to them---the entry in the club suit itself.

East can tell that a ◊K continuation will be ruffed, for from ◊AK *doubleton*, West would lead the ◊K. That, and king from ace-king-queen, are vital exceptions to the usual rule. So East should *discourage* at Trick 1.

Then it will be up to West to figure out why. West must "see" his one spade and two heart tricks as the setting tricks. If he is alert to the danger, he will attack clubs at Trick 2 and rise with the ♠Q on the first spade to finish the job of removing dummy's club entries. He can wait for his two heart tricks to beat 4♠.

DEAL 161. GET A STEP AHEAD

```
                    ♠ K J 5
                    ♡ A
                    ◇ A 8 7 5 4 2
                    ♣ A 6 4
        ♠ 10 8 4 2                   ♠ A Q 9 3
        ♡ 9 4                        ♡ Q 6 2
        ◇ Q 9 3                      ◇ K J 10
        ♣ Q 8 7 2                    ♣ J 10 9
                    ♠ 7 6
                    ♡ K J 10 8 7 5 3
                    ◇ 6
                    ♣ K 5 3
```

Despite the misfit, North had enough high-card strength to raise South's 3♡ opening to 4♡.

West led the ♠2 to dummy's ♠J and East's ♠Q.

East shifted to the ♣J. South won the ♣K, led to dummy's ◇A and ruffed a diamond, returned to dummy's ♡A and ruffed another Declarer won the king, led a diamond to dummy's ace and ruffed another diamond.

Now dummy's diamonds were high. Declarer cashed the ♡K and dislodged East's ♡Q with his ♡J. With the ♣A still in dummy, East could only cash the ♠A to stop an overtrick.

Could East have *beaten* 4♡?

Yes. Though East appreciated the urgency of removing dummy's entries, he failed to see that the only entry he could remove with certainty at Trick 2 *before declarer could use it* to ruff a diamond was the ♡A.

Lead the ♡2 to Trick 2, and now the defense is one step ahead, or declarer is one step behind. By the time declarer can establish dummy's diamonds, all dummy's entries will be gone.

Nine tricks only, and 4♡ goes down one.

DEAL 162. TAKE AWAY AN ENTRY

```
                  ♠ A K 10 7 5 3
                  ♡ 4
                  ◇ K 9 3
                  ♣ Q 9 2
    ♠ J 4 2                       ♠ Q 9 8
    ♡ 10 9 6 3                    ♡ A K 8 7 5
    ◇ 8 6 5                       ◇ 7
    ♣ K 8 5                       ♣ J 10 7 3
                  ♠ 6
                  ♡ Q J 2
                  ◇ A Q J 10 4 2
                  ♣ A 6 4
```

Some devotees of Two-Over-One Game-Forcing think that when responder has forced to game, they don't need strong jump rebids and can therefore afford to use opener's jump shifts as splinters. This pair proved them wrong. After a 1♠-2◇; 2♠-3◇; 4◇ start, South cue-bid 5♣. Then North jumped to 6◇ *because* he had a singleton heart. Simple!

West led the ♡10 to East's ♡K. East shifted to the ♣J. South didn't think this was an underlead from the ♣K, so he won the ♣A. Needing *two* club discards, he played to set up dummy's spades.

♠AK, spade ruffed high, and with spades 3-3, he drew trump ending in dummy and had 12 tricks. Had spades been 4-2, he could still make 6◇ if he caught a 2-2 trump split.

Could the defenders have prevailed?

Yes. Dummy's third trump was vital for declarer, who needed a trump entry to dummy *after* ruffing out the spades. To kill that entry, East must sacrifice his ♡A at Trick 2.

Declarer gains one trick for his ♡Q and another by ruffing a heart but loses three long spades that he cannot reach to cash after he sets them up.

Down one.

DEAL 163. NOT AGAIN?

```
                    ♠ 8 5 2
                    ♡ K 9 5
                    ◇ K 8
                    ♣ A J 8 5 2
   ♠ K J 7 6                        ♠ Q 10 3
   ♡ 8                              ♡ 7 4
   ◇ 10 7 6 5 3                     ◇ A Q 9 2
   ♣ 7 4 3                          ♣ K Q 10 6
                    ♠ A 9 4
                    ♡ A Q J 10 6 3 2
                    ◇ J 4
                    ♣ 9
```

After North's forcing 1NT response to 1♡, South jumped to 3♡ and North, who had intended bidding 3♡ himself over a minimum rebid, raised to 4♡ and started thinking what dessert he would order with the afternoon's winnings.

West led the ◇5 and followed with the ◇3 as East took the first two diamond tricks. Hoping to catch his partner with spade strength behind declarer, East shifted to the ♠3. South won the ♠A, led to dummy's ♣A, and ruffed three clubs high, using dummy's ♡9 and ♡K for entries.

When clubs split 4-3 and trumps split 3-2, dummy's ♡5 was the entry he needed to reach the fifth club for his tenth trick. 4♡ made and North decided on chocolate mousse pie.

West pulled a cell phone from his pocket to cancel the evening's reservation at Scotch and Sirloin. Then, turning to East, he said, "Didn't we have a deal like this just three rubbers ago? How often must you get it wrong before you get it right?"

What did East do wrong both times?

He neglected a chance to kill a dummy entry before it became useful. By leading the ♡4 to Trick 2, he could force declarer to use a dummy entry prematurely. Dummy's fifth club will go to waste.

West will have steak for dinner and North may abstain from dessert entirely.

DEAL 164. RECOGNITION

```
                        ♠ K 9 6
                        ♡ 9 5 3
                        ◊ A 9 7 5 2
                        ♣ K J
        ♠ Q                             ♠ 7 2
        ♡ Q 10 7 6 2                    ♡ K J
        ◊ J 8 6                         ◊ K Q 10 3
        ♣ 10 9 8 3                      ♣ A Q 6 4 2
                        ♠ A J 10 8 5 4 3
                        ♡ A 8 4
                        ◊ 4
                        ♣ 7 5
```

For lack of a good rebid after a 1♣ opening a 1♡ response, and dissatisfaction with the alternative plan (a 1◊ opening followed by a 2♣

rebid), East opened a slightly flawed 15-17 HCP 1NT. South overcalled a conventional 2◊ showing an unspecified major one-suiter and North replied 2♡, content to stop in a partscore opposite hearts. When South "corrected" to 2♠, North revalued his hand and jumped to 4♠.

West led the ♣10.

East won two club tricks, then shifted to the ♡K. Declarer won and started dummy's side suit: ◊A, diamond ruff. ♠K, felling West's ♠Q, diamond ruff high, ♠8 to dummy's ♠9 and a third diamond ruff high.

Now he led low to dummy's ♠6 to discard a heart on dummy's established ◊9. Making 4♠, losing two clubs and one heart.

Unbeatable? Or could the defenders have prevailed?

As usual, recognizing the deal type could help. Dummy's diamonds loomed as a threat. As usual, the best counter is an attack on dummy's entries. East should see the way, as dummy's only entry to a long diamond can be in trump.

A trump shift at Trick 3 wrecks declarer's timing. He has three trump entries to dummy but must use one prematurely. Dummy's fifth diamond can be set up but not cashed, and 4♠ goes down one.

Printed in the United States
by Baker & Taylor Publisher Services